MONEY MATTERS *for women*

AILEEN F. CASHMAN

First published in 1989 by
Attic Press,
44 East Essex Street,
Dublin 2.

British Library Cataloguing in Publication Data
Cashman, Aileen F.
Money management handbook
1. Personal finance — For women
I. Title
332.024'042

ISBN 0-946211-75-2

Cover Design: McArdle Design
Typesetting: Phototype-Set Ltd., Dublin
Printing: The Guernsey Press Co. Ltd., Guernsey, Channel Islands

DEDICATION

For all my clients
and
my mother

CONTENTS

FOREWORD

WHY AM I ALWAYS WORRYING ABOUT MONEY?

Before I answer this question, let me first ask you if any of the following responses to money worries sound familiar to you:

'The problem will go away.'
'I'll muddle through somehow.'
'Maybe I'll win the lottery.'
'I've no money anyway, so why worry.'
'My partner/spouse will get a promotion.'

Although this may not be your own response to money worries, you will have met these reactions from time to time. What these responses have in common is that they all avoid the issue and none of them realistically do anything to make the worry go away. They also devalue the importance of money by putting it firmly in someone else's control. However, what you can't control is often what you worry about most, so this sort of response will usually lead to a vicious circle of 'worry — non-response — worry'.

To answer the 'why' question above, you should first of all admit that money matters in your life. Then ask yourself how you usually respond to areas of importance. What situations work well for you? What are the things that make you feel bad? Good experiences will probably be those where (a) you have sufficient information to handle the situation, (b) you know what to expect, and (c) you manage and control the situation to bring it to a personally satisfactory conclusion. Good money management works in exactly the same way.

MANAGING YOUR MONEY WELL

To do this you need to understand the main elements involved:

1. Yourself, and how you relate to money.
2. The other players — the financial institutions, how they operate and what they have that you might need or want.
3. The state systems — taxation, law and social welfare.

The aim of this book is to get you to think about and understand yourself, and to give you general guidelines about the other players and the state systems. This information is set in the context of typical situations that you will meet in life.

PLANNING IS ESSENTIAL

Having good information is the first key to controlling your situation, with money as with anything else. The prelude to planning for your future is to be fully aware of your present financial situation and how you have arrived at this point. Then set yourself concrete objectives, defining these objectives as much as possible. Ask questions about the objectives — why?, where?, how much?, and when? The 'when' question puts your objective into a time frame and will highlight the effort necessary to achieve the objective: eg if you want to buy a house within one year at a price of £40,000 and have no savings now, you will have to either save or borrow approximately £6,000-£7,000 in the year to enable you to proceed.

Having set your objectives, identify people and resources which could back you. Try to anticipate practical problems also (ie what could go wrong), but focus more on things that will help rather than hinder you.

Good money management involves handling the present and creating the future by making decisions and taking action now. People seldom just arrive at a point in their lives. The shape of your life now was created by decisions in your past. Taking no decisions or actions is a decision in itself, but will usually lead to problems rather than shaping a future of your own choosing.

Money *matters*, and is often a vital tool in getting you what you want. If you know how it works, you can make it work for you. This will enhance your confidence and add to your sense of independence and security. And don't think that this only applies to women with good incomes or capital behind them. If anything, the woman on very limited means gains most by managing her money. Knowing that she has *decided* how even £1 is spent for her own benefit gives her a sense of control. Women understand how small things mount up. This knowledge, with their skills with people and detail, means that money is an area where women can excel.

HOW TO USE THIS HANDBOOK

This handbook is addressed primarily to women, and is part of a series dealing with topics such as Social Welfare and Women in Business. Where another handbook in the series can help the reader in understanding a situation, I refer to it.

The book is divided into three main sections, broadly according to the stages in a woman's life. Chapters within each Section describe particular financial institutions or situations and set out the information you will need to get the best value for your money.

Section 1 covers budgeting, the banks and other institutions, employment, savings, small borrowing and renting.

Section 2 deals with purchasing a house, marriage (some implications of), protecting your assets, maximising your tax relief and setting up in business.

Section 3 deals with retirement plans, death, separation, and lump sum investments.

The logic of this sequence is that it reflects the order in which you might reasonably expect to meet different life situations. This, however, will not be the case for many individuals so each chapter aims to stand on its own. Because of this, there will inevitably be duplication of information regarding the institutions and state systems, for which I apologise. However, I try to emphasise the particular facet of the institution, law, tax and social system in context, and hope that this is clear to the reader.

SECTION 1: THE EARLY YEARS

BEGIN BY BUDGETING

Budgeting is the start of money management. Your budget is the axle on which your money management wheel turns. The process of budgeting does not depend on whether you have lots of money, or very little; in fact, I have found that people with relatively small amounts of money often budget far more effectively than those who are better off. The latter can fall into the trap of feeling there is no need to watch their day-to-day spending because they have a very good regular income, or have a lot of money to fall back on. This attitude can lead to debt.

Budgeting involves looking at the essentials of your day-to-day spending and setting priorities for what is important. Analyse what you spend your money on and compare this with your income. This will show what room for manoeuvre is available to you.

Basic budgeting involves sitting down with a sheet of paper and putting your income on one side and your outgoings on the other side. Make sure that *all* your outgoings are included. Divide these up among the expenditure which happens monthly, quarterly or annually. When you do this exercise, don't *underestimate* the figures. It is always a good idea to look back through your most recent bills and bank statements to see your exact spending over the last six to twelve months.

On the income side, you will probably be receiving some form of regular income, eg salary from a job, benefit/assistance from Social Welfare, or some other form of regular income. There may also be other things that come in less regularly, eg children's allowance, or sums of money from other forms of employment. You should include these on your income side and then assess your average annual income as precisely as you can. For easier management, break this down by periods such as weekly or monthly income. Table 1 gives a detailed example of a budget exercise.

TELL YOURSELF THE TRUTH!

If you find yourself having great difficulty with a budgeting exercise, it is an indicator of how you feel about managing your money. It may be that you are afraid to look at your expenses because in some way you know you never seem to have any spare cash and are afraid to find out where exactly all the money is going. You may feel that looking at the outgoings will draw you into some other problem, for example the fact that a lot of your outgoings are controlled by somebody else such as family, spouse, or some situation arising from your work. The question to ask yourself at the start of a budgeting exercise is whether you feel that you have a good idea of where your money goes. It is very important to tell yourself the truth about your expenses; there is no point in saying that you only spend £5 a week on entertainment when in fact your cheque book over the last six months shows it was averaging out at £50 a week! *The important thing in the whole budgeting exercise is to see what is actually happening*. At least if you are in possession of full and accurate information, you can decide if this is how you want to spend your money, or whether you would like to change the pattern.

PETTY CASH EXERCISE

It can be a good exercise to undertake a small cash record for a couple of weeks so that you will become aware of your day-to-day expenses. A petty cash exercise involves keeping an exact record of all money spent on a day-to-day basis, for about one month. You *must write every single thing down*, all cheques, all cash expenses, and any credit card expenses. If you do this for one month, you will get a good idea of where the money is

TABLE 1 — INCOME

INCOME	Weekly	Monthly	Annual	OUTGOINGS — ALL	Weekly	Monthly	2 Monthly	Quarterly	Annual
SELF				**FIXED**					
Wages/Salary				Rent					
Fees				Mortgage					
Social Welfare				Bank Loan/Credit Union					
Other				House Insurance					
				Contents/Insurance					
Partner				Life Assurance					
Wages/Salary				VHI					
Fees				Car Insurance					
Social Welfare				Car Tax					
Other				TV Licence					
				TV Cable					
OTHERS				Ground Rent					
Wages/Salary				Child Minder/House Keeper					
Fees				House Keeper					
Social Welfare				**REGULAR**					
Other				ESB					
				Phone					
				Gas					
				Oil/Fuel					
				Petrol					
				Transport					
				Car Service					
				Food — Home					
				Food — Work					
				Subscriptions					
				VARIABLE					
				Clothes					
				Holidays					
				House Maintenance					
				Fees					
				Christmas					
				Discretionary					
				ie Entertainment					
Totals									
Surplus/Deficit									

going. When you analyse the expenses, you can find whether there is much more than you thought going in a certain direction, or whether in fact the money is all going on things that are essential. This type of exercise can be very important when your financial situation is about to change, or perhaps your income is likely to decrease. For example, people going into retirement from employment will usually experience a real drop in income. To decide how to cope with this drop in income, you need to have a very good idea of how your money is being spent now.

SUMMARY

- Include everything — all income and all outgoings.
- Be realistic — check your *outgoings* particularly.
- Keep records — cheques, cash and credit cards.
- Check your outgoings against your priorities — is this how you *want* to spend your money?
- How much, if any, spare capacity have you?
- If you have spare cash after all the essentials, ask yourself what you want this to do for you.
- Set objectives for your spending, most of which will relate to short-term needs but, if you can, make your money work for your future also.

KNOW YOUR FINANCIAL INSTITUTIONS

All through your life, you will be dealing with some or all of the financial institutions. Money 'movement' is now highly automated and more and more paper and cash transactions are being computerised. You can have your income paid direct to your bank, and have savings deducted from your bank account by direct debit mandate or standing order. You can also pay bills through cash machines, by cash or cheque, and for larger purchases cheque and credit/charge cards are almost essential.

Day-to-day money management aims to have your income and outgoings operated automatically and evenly over manageable periods, eg monthly, quarterly, etc. It should also ensure that the priorities and objectives you set yourself are reflected in your management system, and that the essentials and desirables work automatically: mortgage payments and car insurance on standing order ex current account; holiday savings moving to an interest earning account by standing order each month. Throughout the year this type of system leaves you with a clear monthly or weekly balance for day-to-day spending, having catered for the less immediate needs. And what if your income is not sufficient to meet your outgoings? Then you will need to know what credit may be available to you. How will the institutions assess you if you need credit? What are their considerations and what will it cost?

Unless you choose to operate solely in cash (which will mean a lot of work for you, together with a security risk and poor returns on your money) you should set up a management system which enables you to deal easily with financial situations. This means using the *current account, savings account and lending facilities* of the financial institutions.

BANKS

The Associated Banks offer a wide range of services and facilities, eg current accounts, secured and unsecured loans, loans accounts, savings accounts, credit cards, bank drafts, cash machines, automatic transactions.

The banks regulate the flow of money in the economy, and

you will need many of their services to make your money work. There are charges for their services, and a large proportion of their income comes from their lending operations. Examine their accounts, costs and facilities and find the combination to suit you personally. Ease of management and short-term credit facilities are their strong features, and it is advisable to establish a relationship with your bank early in your financial life. Remember, however, that they vary in their costs and facilities, so shop around. There is also strong competition between them to obtain customers, so if you're not happy you can consider switching, either to a different branch or to a different bank. Often you will find that it is the bank manager and not the institution that makes the difference.

Deposit Account

This is a bank savings account where you can make cash or cheque lodgements and withdraw money, usually in cash. You can arrange for standing orders to be paid from a deposit account, and will earn interest on your savings on a daily basis. Normal bank charges do not usually apply to deposit accounts. Unfortunately, the rate of interest is at present very low and *deposit retention tax* is also deducted from the interest earned on savings. It is now possible to operate a cash card on a deposit account, which means you can use the Automatic Teller Machines (ATM) available in your bank's branches. This means you can get at your money almost all of the time, whereas previously you could only withdraw funds during normal banking hours.

Cashsave/Pass Account

This is similar to a deposit account and mainly functions through the ATM machines. A variation in facilities on this account, as distinct from the normal deposit account, is that it will allow you to operate direct debits from it, unlike some deposit accounts which only accept standing orders. Whenever you are opening an account, check what type of instructions it will accept, eg standing orders or direct debits, as these facilities could be useful to you at some stage in the future. With cash accounts, you have the facility on some of them to check your present balance, pay bills, and make lodgements. A point to bear in mind with these accounts is that transactions which are carried out through ATMs are frequently the cheapest. You may also earn interest on your money, and can have your salary paid direct to this account.

Current Account

This is the account which gives you the facility of a cheque book and usually a cheque guarantee card, and is probably the most familiar of all accounts to bank customers. You make lodgements and withdrawals, either by cash or cheque, and interest is not payable on credit balances, although you will be charged interest if your account is overdrawn. This account accepts either direct debit or standing order instructions and it is also possible to obtain a cash card. This means that your money is accessible to you and that you can undertake all the ATM transactions which I mentioned in the previous paragraph. Perhaps the most significant feature of a current account is that you can arrange an overdraft facility on it. This basically means that the bank can fund you if you find yourself short of cash. However, you should remember that an overdraft facility should be negotiated and also agreed with your bank. I will discuss this in more detail in Chapter 5.

Standing Order

The use of standing order instructions on your bank account can be a very good strategy to ensure that money is set aside to meet present and future requirements. For instance, where you are trying to budget for bills spread over a full year, I would recommend that you arrange a monthly standing order from your current account to a savings account so that the budget for bills is taken out at an even amount throughout the year. The banks now utilise this concept in their budget saver and masterplan type accounts. However, unless you need an overdraft as part of your bills/budget arrangement, I would recommend that you save this money in a deposit account, preferably with a building society, where the interest is better. In that way your money will be working for you while it is building up to meet bills throughout the year. The important thing about the standing order is that it makes money move automatically, and this is why it is so effective.

Other Banking Services

The banks offer a range of other services such as safe deposit boxes, student services, trustees arrangements, and the provision of travellers' cheques and bank drafts for customers. They also offer *free banking* in respect of certain types of accounts kept in credit and for customers aged over 55. It is important to remember that there really is no such thing as free banking. What is really meant here is 'free if in credit' banking. Check with your particular bank what their minimum balance requirements are, and the charging period, to see if you can avail of free banking.

Bank Charges

An important point to keep in mind when dealing with the banks is that they are profit-making organisations and operate on a commercial basis. Although they have the use of your money while it is in their hands, they charge for many of their services. You should be aware of the differences that exist between different banks in respect of charges.

Dealing with your Bank

An important point to consider when dealing with the bank is the degree of efficiency at your particular branch. I recommend that any instruction you give to a bank be put in writing as communication by telephone can sometimes go astray. Always check your bank statements when they arrive to ensure that the various instructions you have given are being carried out. I would also advise that you obtain *monthly bank statements* on your main accounts as this makes it much easier to check the various transactions than if the statements are only received on a quarterly basis. It is an excellent idea to build up a good relationship with your bank as you may well require their services for loans in the future, as well as for the normal day-to-day transactions.

THE POST OFFICE

The post office has branches all over the country. It is a savings institution which is government-backed and extremely secure. The normal post office account is for savings and does not offer any credit facilities, but the post office offers a range of financial services and is open much longer hours than those of banks. This makes it more accessible to many people. (However, ATMs have dramatically improved the banks' standing in this area.)

You can arrange for standing orders to be made to your post office savings account, and you may be able to set up national instalment savings deductions from your salary; such schemes operate for post office staff, teachers, etc. (Details of the conditions and returns on national instalment schemes are given in Chapter 4.) The rate of interest available on post office deposits is better than bank rates for smaller deposits, and money is usually withdrawn either by cash or by money order.

In terms of *medium-term savings/investment,* the post office offers a range of products with three to five year terms which have the benefit of guaranteed returns, and are also free of tax. If you find yourself with a lump sum of money, it could be worth your while to consider the post office. I will outline how these medium-term investments work in Chapters 4 and 15.

BUILDING SOCIETIES

Building Societies were primarily savings and mortgages (loans on assets) institutions but they are now moving into more generalised secured lending. In the future, they hope to offer very similar services to the banks. At the moment, they offer a range of savings accounts and mortgages on domestic and commercial properties.

Mortgages

A mortgage is a loan secured on a property. Up to 90% of the value of a domestic property, and up to 70% of a commercial property, may be mortgaged. When you hold a reasonable net equity in a property, ie the value less any loan outstanding, you may also be able to top-up the original mortgage. This will depend on your ability to repay the new amount and cannot exceed the overall mortgage limits.

Ordinary Share Account

This is a savings account where money is on immediate access, but larger sums of money require notice of withdrawal. Interest is credited on these accounts and is subject to deposit retention tax as with the banks and post office. However, interest with the building society is significantly higher than that available on medium-sized bank deposits. There are many branches of the larger building societies spread all over the country and opening hours are very good; some open on Saturday mornings. However, only one building society operates a cash dispenser machine at the moment.

Lodgements

Lodgements can be made to a building society account either

by hand or by standing order from your bank. A small drawback with building societies is that it can take a long time for cheque lodgements to clear. If you find yourself needing your savings very shortly after you have made a cheque lodgement, you may find that the cash has not been credited to your account and in some instances it has been known to take as long as ten days.

Non-Resident Accounts

In common with the banks, building societies offer non-resident savings accounts for people who may wish to have savings in Ireland but are resident elsewhere. The tax treatment of these accounts is different from that of the normal savings account. The saver makes a non-resident declaration and is exempted from paying deposit retention tax. This is because non-residents are not usually liable to Irish income tax.

Other Building Society Accounts

Building societies offer *fixed term accounts*, where money is put on deposit for a specific period of time, usually three months. A more favourable rate of interest will be paid on this type of savings, with the interest rate increasing depending on the sum of money that is involved. *Monthly income accounts* are also available, where interest is paid by cheque to the saver each month. The minimum balance required to be eligible for fixed term and/or monthly income accounts is usually £3,000-£5,000. Another facility that building societies offer is employee deduction schemes, whereby an employer can arrange for savings to be deducted from salaries and remitted to a building society. Usually, there must be a minimum number of people involved in the scheme and each of these will be issued with a pass book as with a normal share account.

OTHER FINANCIAL INSTITUTIONS

TSB/Cork and Limerick Savings Banks

These savings banks are non-profit-making and are effectively state-guaranteed. They offer ordinary deposit accounts as well as an investment account, which pays a rate of return similar to that of the building societies and requires one month's notice for withdrawal. Current accounts, term loans and mortgages are also available. The range of services and facilities is similar to those of the Associated Banks.

Commercial Banks

These institutions offer business loans and also pay competitive interest rates on deposit accounts. Usually, the minimum deposit required to invest will be £1,000 plus, and money may be placed on fixed term deposit which offers a good rate of interest over the term selected, eg one, three, six or twelve months. Current account facilities are not usually available from Commercial Banks.

Credit Unions

Credit unions differ quite significantly from the other financial institutions in that they are non-profit-making. Their members share what is known as a *common bond.* This means that members either live in the same area, or share a common bond of having the same employer.

Credit unions offer savings which are expressed in terms of shares, and earn interest in the form of a dividend. Dividends represent the profit made by the credit union, after deduction of expenses. Deposit retention tax is not deducted from dividends and information on dividends paid to members is returned to the Revenue Commissioners. These dividends or the interest tend to be quite low, but on the other hand they offer low-cost borrowing; for many people this is the main advantage of being a member of a credit union.

SUMMARY

- Establish a relationship with your bank.
- Open a building society account for savings.
- Have your income lodged directly to your bank, if possible.
- Arrange standing orders/direct debits from your bank for bills and savings.
- Consider opening a credit union savings account.

YOUR INCOME — HOW MUCH YOU REALLY EARN

I will now outline some general employment considerations and how you can expect income to operate from employment and from other sources, eg social welfare or self-employment. I set out the range of deductions you can encounter in paid employment, and briefly discuss tax and PRSI deductions.

INCOME FROM EMPLOYMENT

Letter of Appointment

When you take up an offer of employment, you will usually receive a letter of appointment. With larger organisations, there may also be a booklet giving details of all the employee benefits. Your letter of appointment will usually state your gross salary per annum; how this is payable, eg monthly, weekly, the method of payment, eg cheque, cash or credit transfer; the nature of your appointment, eg temporary, permanent or part-time; and any special conditions that may apply to your appointment, eg six months probationary period, salary review each year, etc.

Employee Benefits

Employee benefits that have a direct financial impact on your income are sick pay, holidays, paid or unpaid leave, pension provisions, income protection, and 'perks' like low interest loans, VHI paid for by the company, company cars, etc. The important thing is to know your entitlements and the procedures involved if you need to call upon them. For example, if you are sick, how soon do you have to produce a medical certificate? How long will the company pay you? How are you to obtain payment thereafter? Are you expected to draw social welfare disability benefit and repay this to the company? Financial benefits which a company may offer, such as a pension, income protection, and life assurance, are often less well understood than matters such as sick pay. This is because the situation is less immediate. It is also because the area appears to be more complex and is more at the discretion of the employer, whereas sick pay is usually covered by legislation.

In the early stages of employment, when you are under 25 and perhaps single, the issues of pension and life assurance may seem less than relevant. However, sickness cover for a long-term disability can be important at any age, so you should check with your employer whether this is part of your employment package.

After your mid-twenties pension becomes relevant, as it requires a long investment, typically 30 to 40 years, to provide meaningful and attractive benefits. If your employer has a scheme, check the conditions on it to see what your entitlement would be if you join. Convert that entitlement from a future picture to present-day terms and see whether this might be sufficient for you to live on. A common idea that people have is that once there is a company pension scheme, employees are automatically entitled to adequate pension. This is not necessarily the case, and only a small number of company schemes provide for maximum pension benefits as allowed by the Revenue Commissioners. Examine your own scheme carefully — you may decide that you could do better yourself by organising your own pension, or you may need to supplement the company scheme by some additional savings.

Salary Deductions

As anyone knows who is in employment, your gross salary can bear little resemblance to your actual take-home pay when all the usual deductions are made. The largest deduction is tax, so you need to understand something about the PAYE system (pay as you earn) and how it works in relation to your employment.

PAYE/PRSI

If you've never worked before, you (not your employer) need to *register for tax and for PRSI and request a tax-free allowance*, which is what your employer will use when deducting tax from you. If you do not have a tax-free allowance in respect of your employment, your employer will be obliged to operate emergency tax deductions until such time as the appropriate tax-free allowance is received. The tax-free allowance will state that your allowances in respect of your employment with company X are £Y per annum. It will also state whether the allowances are to be divided evenly over 52 weeks or whether you can earn up to a certain amount before starting to pay tax. Everyone who has taxable income is entitled to a personal tax-free allowance, and if you are taxed under PAYE you should also have a PAYE allowance. Table 2 gives details of current and proposed basic tax-free allowances, and also outlines the rates of tax on different levels of income.

As well as tax, the other standard deduction is *Pay Related Social Insurance (PRSI)*. Most people pay social insurance at the A1 rate which is at present 7.75% of your gross salary up to £16,700 pa and 1% on income over this amount. However, anyone in the public service will usually pay a lower rate of PRSI, ie 3.15%, which will only qualify them for very limited benefits, ie contributory widow's or orphan's pension, deserted wife's benefits and occupational injuries. If you pay the A1 rate of PRSI, you should have a PRSI tax-free allowance of £286 per annum. You don't get this if you pay reduced-rate PRSI.

TABLE 2 — TAX BANDS PLUS ALLOWANCES
TAX BANDS

	1989/90		1988/89
Proposed Tax rates	Bands *Single/Married	Existing Tax rate	Bands *Single/Married
32%	6,100/12,200	35%	5,700/11,400
48%	3,100/6,200	48%	2,900/6,800
56%	Balance	58%	Balance

*Single includes widowed

Personal Allowances

Allowance:	1989/90	1988/89
Single person:	2,050	2,050
Married person:	4,100	4,100
Widowed person:	2,550	2,550
Widow bereaved in year of assessment (assumed)	4,100	4,100
One parent family allowance:		
(i) Widowed person	1,550	1,550
(ii) Other persons	2,050	2,050
Age allowance:		
(i) Single/Widowed	200	200
(ii) Married:	400	400
Incapacitated child allowance:	600	600
Child allowance for 'qualifying low income families'		
Allowance per child	200	Nil
PAYE allowance:	800	800
PRSI allowance (for employees only):	286	286

Leaving Work

When you leave a job, you will receive a *P45* from your ex-employer. This states the tax-free allowance the previous employer operated, the tax paid to date of leaving work and the PRSI paid. You give a copy of this to your new employer and you apply for a new tax-free allowance certificate in respect of your new employment. The P45 form is very important and you should always get one when you leave employment, even if you are not taking up another job. In the event of your not taking up another job, you will need your P45 to reclaim any tax that you may have overpaid.

The other form that you will receive in employment is a *P60*, which is the year end statement of your total salary and the tax and PRSI that you have paid to that year end, which is usually 5 April. When you complete your tax returns, you should send a copy of this with your tax form so that the Revenue Commissioners can see what tax you've paid and whether there are any over- or under-payments.

Other Salary Deductions

As well as the usual tax and PRSI, with the employee's authorisation and the agreement of the employer, many different deductions can be made from your salary. Some typical examples are pensions, life assurance, building society savings, credit union loans and savings, company loans, VHI, and union memberships.

For an employer to operate a salary deduction scheme, there must usually be a minimum number of employees involved, for example ten or twenty. However, minimum numbers required by the organisation to whom the deductions are payable, eg the VHI, are usually quite small — about ten. Therefore, once the minimum membership is met, the only other requirement is to get the employer to administer the deductions.

Other Employee Benefits

Company cars, expenses, VHI, shares and low interest loans are all possible benefits that you might have from your employment. There are tax implications to receiving these types of benefits, and in the case of company cars, low interest loans, VHI and shares, there will usually be a benefit-in-kind deduction from your tax-free allowances. Despite this benefit-in-kind taxation, the advantage of the benefit will usually outweigh the deduction in tax-free allowances. For low interest mortgages, the rate of interest used to calculate the benefit-in-kind has dropped from 12% to 10% following the 1989 budget. This is a welcome adjustment and is more realistic in the light of current interest rates. The payment of expenses to employees in respect of allowable costs incurred on behalf of the company is not subject to income tax or benefit-in-kind assessment.

Social Welfare Income

In money management terms, this income will usually be

very low so your spending and choices will be very restricted. See whether you can open any accounts with the financial institutions mentioned in the first section, and whether you can use their systems to manage your money for you. Try to budget and prioritise your spending to cover your most important day-to-day needs, while still not ignoring, if possible, less immediate financial risk provisions such as house and life assurance. You should also look at credit unions which offer budgeting accounts and cheap loans. Credit unions are less likely than banks to see you as a 'poor risk' in lending terms. This could be important to your overall cash management situation, as your social welfare income will only, in itself, be sufficient for 'poverty-line' existence. *Social Welfare for Women*, another handbook in this series, provides more detailed information.

Self-Employed Income

In the early stages of your financial life, you are less likely to have a self-employed income. However, remember that all taxable income must be returned to the Revenue Commissioners, for example deposit interest, income from a trade or fees — even where some deductions for tax (eg DIRT) have been made. In money management terms, someone with self-employed income needs to be very well organised. Their income may not be regular, and when it arrives will have to be planned to provide for present needs and future outgoings, particularly tax and PRSI.

SUMMARY

- Know the general conditions relating to your income - either salary, or social welfare. These conditions can have financial implications for you, eg (a) sick pay/disability income/pensions, (b) credits for social welfare benefits received from signing on, even if no payment is due to you.
- Understand how standard deductions operate from your income, ie tax and PRSI.
- See if you can arrange non-standard deductions from your salary to provide for savings and risk benefits, eg building society/post office savings, VHI, life assurance etc.
- Even if your income is very low, as with social welfare, investigate whether any of the financial institutions can help you manage it, or can supplement your income through low-cost lending.
- If all your income is from self-employment, and comes in irregularly, you must budget annually. Don't forget about tax and PRSI.

SAVINGS (SHORT-TERM AND MEDIUM-TERM)

From an early age, you will have cash needs for which your regular income is insufficient. When you are faced with this situation, there are basically three options:

1. You have planned for the situation and have been putting money aside. Therefore you have cash available.
2. You have a Fairy Godmother who gives you the cash that you need.
3. You borrow it.

Most of us will have recourse to all three options as we go through life, but realistically we usually operate on some sort of a mix of options 1 and 3 above — option 2 is a rare occurrence! A very important factor which influences how you address your need for cash is *the time you have to plan for the situation.* Naturally, if something comes up at short notice, like a special holiday or an emergency, you are less likely to have planned for it. In this instance, you may have to borrow.

Certain types of borrowing can actually make very good sense because of tax relief, and because they allow you to have access to goods or a lifestyle or education which you can pay back for over time. (See Chapter 5)

In managing your money, you want it to work for you now, and at the same time to protect you against nasty financial shocks in the future. You will also want to be able to avail of opportunities which involve expenditure, be they large or small. Almost everyone, therefore, has some need to save.

Saving Regularly

It goes without saying that to save you must have some spare cash. If you have examined your income and outgoings, you will know whether you have any unallocated cash after providing for all your day-to-day needs. Early in your life, there are usually fewer demands on your income and this can be a very good time to learn how to save. *The golden rule to success in saving is to make it happen automatically.* Even when someone is very good at managing their day-to-day cash, savings, which are of their nature discretionary and less immediate, will tend to get put aside in favour of more urgent spending. So if you've decided you want to save, organise it on standing order, by way of salary deduction, or on a direct debit.

With the array of savings products that are available, and

with so much competition for savers' money, it can be difficult to decide on the best place to save. In choosing the savings product for you, *time, risk, rate of return* and the *accessibility of your savings* are the important factors to keep in mind. The longer the time you want to save for, the broader your choice of savings vehicles. If you want your money to be totally accessible to you, your choice will be more limited. And if you want guarantees on the security of your savings and on the rate of return, you will only have a few options. The rate of return you can get for your money is strongly affected by the risk you want to take and by taxation.

Taxation is a 'given' in the savings situation, ie either it applies or it does not. Risk, however, is more subjective, but you should aim to spread and minimise your risk, while still earning reasonable returns.

In planned savings, you should cater for short-term needs first, then medium- and longer-term requirements. Identify specific things that you want or need to save for, eg car insurance (short-term), setting up in business in seven to ten years (medium-term), early retirement (long-term). Then look at the savings products available and make sure that the one you choose is suitable to your personal objective.

As well as organising your savings on a regular basis to provide whatever cash sum you require, you should keep an eye on any lump sums created by regular savings. A lump sum in this case can be anything from £1,000 plus. With lump sums, your timescale for investment changes, and generally you can adopt three to five years planning cycles for larger cash amounts. To create those in the first place may take you five to ten years. Lump sums can work harder for you and faster than smaller regular savings. This chapter relates to regular savings, ie how to create a lump sum. Chapter 13 will set out your money-making options once you have a lump sum.

SHORT-TERM SAVINGS

If you're likely to need your savings *on demand*, the building society is probably the best place, as the interest here is usually better than the banks or the post office. You will pay DIRT on most deposits but your cash will be readily available to you.

Fixed Term Savings

If you find that your money sits for six to twelve months after you have saved it before you have need of the funds, you should consider fixed term accounts, or post office savings products, some of which are tax-free. The minimum deposit required for fixed term accounts ranges from £10 (post office) to £3,000 (building society). With all savings where you commit to a fixed term, eg one month, six months, etc, you should time your withdrawals carefully to avoid any loss of interest between terms. For example, with PO savings certificates, interest is only added at six-monthly intervals, so money withdrawn between six-monthly intervals will not earn interest at all.

SUMMARY: SHORT-TERM SAVINGS

- are savings where the money will be required within a specific period, but particularly within 1-36 months;
- offer capital guarantees;
- can offer fixed returns over specified periods;
- can be tax efficient for high taxpayers, eg post office returns on savings certificates;
- suit small or large regular savings.

MEDIUM-TERM SAVINGS

If you are saving with a longer time-frame in mind, ie four to ten years, your range of savings options increase. All the options covered previously are available to you, but you should also consider some investment type of savings as well. Returns on investment-type savings are higher than those from the post office or building societies in the six to ten year period. However, as these are investments, there is a different degree of risk involved which is why they earn more.

Savings or Investments?

If you are putting money aside into some sort of savings account, you need to have a clear understanding of whether interest is being added to your savings each month, or whether your savings are being invested with a view to capital growth. *In ideal savings terms, you should have a mixture of both types*, as they address different needs and time-spans. However, it is extremely important to understand the difference between them.

Fixed interest savings, such as banks, building societies, post offices, and government securities, tell you precisely how much you are going to earn if you save with them under certain conditions. For instance, if you buy £1 of government stock for £1, at a rate of interest of ½%, you will know that every year you will earn ½% on that £1 investment (you will be liable to tax on this interest). On the redemption date (say October 1992), your investment of £1 will be returned to you so you know exactly what is going to happen if you hold the investment until a specified date.

Savings which are invested for capital growth, on the other hand, do not tell you how much you will make and the form of your return is different. These types of savings are more like the situation where a person buys a house and subsequently sells it at a profit. The return on the investment is what is known as *capital gain.*

Fixed Interest Savings

All the products appropriate for short-term savings can be used to save for the medium-term, ie banks, building societies, and the post office savings certificates and bonds. Your savings are very secure but your returns will be quite low; so don't put all your money into this type of savings, *unless* you want to avoid risk completely.

National Instalment Savings Schemes

The national instalment savings scheme is available to any individual who wishes to set up a regular savings contract with An Post. The saver undertakes to put aside between £5 and £150 per month for twelve months. At the end of the twelve instalments, the money saved will be placed on deposit for periods ranging from one to five years. Returns on national instalments are guaranteed and can be adjusted for inflation. The following returns are available currently:

At end of year 2	8%
At end of year 3	17%
At end of year 4	28%
At end of year 5	39%
At end of year 6	50%

A number of points need to be kept in mind regarding national instalment savings schemes:

1. The total interest is only paid when you withdraw your money, and you should remember that there is no interest paid at all in the first year.
2. You can miss a monthly payment and continue with your scheme but you must then make a full total of twelve payments before you earn interest.
3. If you miss two payments, you must withdraw from the scheme, and will not earn any interest on your savings.
4. Where national instalment savings are cashed in other than at yearly intervals after the final instalment is paid, returns shown are paid with the interest at the ordinary post office savings rate for each extra *complete* month of investment.

5. Returns quoted above include the 5% bonus payable at the end of year 6.

Investment-Type Savings Investment-type savings are usually referred to as life assurance linked savings and can be structured to provide for your full life assurance requirements, or to provide minimum assurance and maximum savings.

The minimum term which you can select is usually ten years: and you can also decide to save for longer, eg 15 — 20 — 25 years, as perhaps with retirement planning.

The life assurance companies are investment companies who invest your savings, after charges and life assurance costs, and manage the money on your behalf. The investment manager manages different pools of money according to the risk and rate-of-return needs of the investors. Taxes are paid within the investment funds and no further tax liability arises to you when you encash your investment.

The return on your investment can be expressed in one of two forms, ie unit-linked or 'with profit'.

Unit-linked investment describes your savings as being worth so many units at a particular price and varies from day-to-day. 'With profit', on the other hand, describes your investment in terms of bonuses/dividends which are added to the value of your policy each year per £1000 sum assured. Once added, provided you keep savings for the agreed period, these bonuses cannot be withdrawn. Returns of a 'with profit' nature are therefore *less* subject to wide fluctuation over the term of the policy and provide certain minimum guarantees, eg you will get back the sum invested at the end of x number of years.

Unit-linked returns vary more widely and provide no guarantees. The timing of your encashment therefore would need to be monitored according to unit prices. However, the full return on your investment is paid to you with unit linking, whereas bonuses on 'with profit' policies are at the discretion of the investment company. Unit-linked policies tend to offer more flexibility to the saver and you can also choose the underlying investment, eg property, shares, cash, or some mixture of these. In 'with profit' policies the investment choice is left to the investment manager.

Investment-type savings are medium-term by design and you should be reasonably sure that you will be able to save for the term selected. *Never think that because a policy acquires an encashment value in one or two years that this means that you will get your money back — you won't.* To break even, ie get back the net money you have saved, you should maintain a policy for between one-third to one-half of the selected term. After this your returns will be pure profit, so your final rate of return on investment will vary according to how long you have managed to save. Where the savings are run to maturity, they consistently offer better returns than banks, building societies or the post office.

So why not invest directly, rather than pooling your money and investing via the life assurance companies? For the small regular saver, this option will not be available, as direct investment requires much larger sums of money. In addition, your investment risk is greatly reduced by pooling your money and you are also availing of day-to-day professional management. You can invest in a range of investments as well as one particular type, and the tax advantages of this type of savings are significant. At present, you can qualify for tax relief on half your annual premiums at your highest rate of tax, subject to an overall restriction of £400 pa relief for single people and £800 pa relief for married couples. In addition, any return on investment that you make is free of income and capital gains tax.

SUMMARY — MEDIUM-TERM SAVINGS

- Have a mixture of fixed interest and investment-type savings.
- Watch your timing on fixed term deposits, eg post office certificates, bonds and national instalment savings.
- Be aware of how investment-type savings work and in particular of real returns in the early part of the policy. Investment-type savings should ideally be run to maturity, usually 10 years plus.
- Allocate an 'always affordable' amount for this type of savings.

CREDIT AND BORROWING

There are constant offers in all the media of credit, loans, mortgages, etc. Lending is a big part of the business of many of the financial institutions, and the interest you pay is how they make their money. They are always on the lookout for good customers, but don't let the ready availability of loans hide the actual cost of what you are buying.

Interest rates vary very widely so always check what is known as the *APR — the annual percentage rate*, which is the true cost of borrowing, and try and get the cheapest rate available.

PLASTIC CARDS

Credit in most people's minds means being in a position to obtain goods or services without having to pay for them immediately. Even when writing cheques, there can be a small element of credit in that it can take a few days for a cheque to clear before the money comes out of your account. For many people, however, credit means their use of credit, charge, or store cards.

The two main *credit cards* used in Ireland are Visa and Access which are operated by the leading banks, ie AIB/TSB are the agents for Visa card, while Bank of Ireland/Ulster Bank/National Irish Bank are the agents for Access.

You can use your card to buy goods or services and you will be issued with a statement each month. Usually you have 25 days to pay before interest becomes chargeable.

The important thing to remember about credit cards is that the interest rate on them is very high, ie between 19.5% (NIB) and 24.6% (TSB) per annum. If you find your bill is too high at the end of the month to clear completely, consider using an agreed overdraft arrangement with the bank to clear the credit card balance — the bank interest rate is cheaper. The other cost of a credit card is the government levy of £10. Avoid using them for cash withdrawals, as interest is payable from withdrawal, and pay your bills on time — that way your interest charges should be nil.

Charge cards do not offer long-term credit; you *must* pay off your charge card each month, and if you don't there will be a late payment fee. Another cost of a charge card is that you have to pay a joining fee and a yearly charge; usually, if you wish to have an extra card on your account you will have to pay for this too. There is no credit limit, so you can spend as much as you want — as long as you're prepared to pay it off each month. The main charge cards are the American Express card which is widely accepted, with a joining fee of £10 and a yearly fee of £27.50, and the Diners Club International card, joining fee £15 (although sometimes this need not apply) and a yearly fee of £27.50.

The main advantage of both credit and charge cards is that they are widely acceptable and offer approximately one month's credit on purchases and services paid for by this method. When you get these cards, decide *to use them for specific things*, ie petrol, travel, clothes, etc, and try and keep your credit limit at a reasonable size.

A point to watch about credit cards is the relatively newer facility of using them to pay regular bills, eg the telephone. Unless you have consciously specified in your own mind that you will pay the telephone bill by this method, I would avoid paying regular bills by credit card. By adding regular bills to your credit card spending, you are changing the nature of the expense from a 'bill' to a potential 'debt'.

Store cards can be compared to either credit or charge cards. There are three main types of account:

Budget accounts — these cards are operated by the Switzers group (Moons, Cashes), Brown Thomas and Best's. They are like revolving credit cards and interest is charged from payment rather than statement date.

Monthly accounts — these are like charge cards and effectively the bill must be paid off at the end of each month, but with the advantage that the card is free.

Option accounts — these accounts operate like credit cards and will charge interest on the outstanding balance. However, the card is free here also.

The advantage of store cards is that, unlike credit cards and charge cards, there is no cost to joining, neither is there any government levy on their use. The disadvantage is that the cards restrict you to shopping at the particular store in question. Like credit cards, the annual percentage rate on store cards is very high.

SUMMARY — PLASTIC

- With credit cards, if you want to avoid interest, don't use them for cash withdrawals and pay your outstanding balance in full, and on time.
- If you can be sure of having funds at the end of a month, your credit card is cheaper to use than a cheque book — there are no charges for transactions.
- Keep your credit limit at a figure you can afford. Remember, it can be reduced as well as increased.
- Avoid putting utility bills on your credit card, eg telephone, unless you have decided to do this well in advance and will clear the balance by the due date.
- Don't leave large balances outstanding on credit or charge cards, as the interest costs are very high.
- If you can't clear the amount owed in full each month, consider using an overdraft facility to clear it, as the interest rate is cheaper.
- If you find your credit card spending getting out of control, go back to using 'real money', ie cash.

BANK LOANS

If you need funds for which your regular income is not sufficient, you will probably find yourself turning to the bank for either an overdraft or a loan. To understand the thinking of the commercial lending institutions, there are a few concepts you should keep in mind:

1. The main concept used by the banks in deciding whether to give you money or not is that of *risk*. Basically, they want to assure themselves that you are a good bet and will pay off the money on the agreed basis.
2. Risk is closely linked to your *ability to pay*, so they will assess your regular income and outgoings to see whether there is room in your budget to repay the loan and the costs involved.
3. For certain types of loans, *security* may be required and this security can vary from a charge on the asset for which the loan was obtained to having your regular income come into your bank account on credit transfer every week or month.

When considering undertaking a loan, always ask for the APR (annual percentage rate) and aim to get the lowest rate possible. If security is required on a loan, try and give the minimum level of security required. Remember that any asset that is assigned to a lender by way of security against a loan can be proceeded against in the event of non-payment.

For certain people, particularly those not in paid employment, or in receipt of social welfare payments, it can be extremely hard to gain access to bank credit or lending facilities. However, if you are a bank customer you should at least talk to your branch manager and ask whether credit facilities will be available to you. Then at least you will know what credit you could hope to receive, should you find yourself in the situation where you need to borrow.

The main types of loans are *overdrafts, term loans, and finance house loans*. These differ from each other as to the true rate of interest that is charged, how it is charged, and suitability for different types of cash flow requirements.

OVERDRAFTS

This is usually the cheapest form of lending and is normally short-term in nature. It is negotiated for a specific period, ie six to twelve months, and you are required to have your account in credit for a minimum of 30 days during the year. Interest is calculated on the daily balance overdrawn and is charged quarterly. An overdraft facility is most suitable for an account that moves regularly from credit to debit, ie black to red. You will find that if you are constantly in the red, the bank will tend to convert the overdraft to a term loan, where repayments must be made monthly. Present APR ranges from 13.5-15.5% for personal customers.

Term Loans

This is an advance of money for a specified purpose, eg fees, holidays, cars, repayable by fixed amounts over an agreed period, usually one to five years, less commonly up to seven years. Repayments are usually made by standing order from your current account and interest is charged on the declining balance, which means that interest is only due on the amount of the loan outstanding from month to month. You can clear a term loan at any stage or reduce it without any penalties. When requesting a term loan, the bank will usually assess your other financial commitments and may ask you for security against the loan. The interest rate charged will depend on the purpose of the loan and whether it is secured or unsecured. Present rates range from 13.5-18%.

Finance House Loans

These are usually unsecured loans. Interest charges (APR) are high and the loan operates differently from term loans from the associated bank. A finance house offers you a loan for a fixed term, for instance one to three years, and interest is calculated at a certain rate on the original amount for the full period of the contract, eg £1,000 at 8% per annum multiplied by three years equals interest of £240 payable. What is often unclear about these loans is that in the early part of the loan the payments are almost all interest. (In the example mentioned, you would be making payments for seven months before starting into the principal sum).

CREDIT UNION LOANS

Credit unions differ significantly from the other financial institutions in that they do not operate on a commercial basis but rather on the basis of thrift and self-help. Essentially, a credit union is a society which has members who are joined by a particular bond. To become a member you simply complete an application form, pay a small entrance fee, and purchase a share. The only people who can borrow from a credit union are its members. Loans may be granted for any good purchase if you can show that you have a need and if you can prove your ability and intent to pay. The size of the loan will be a multiple of your savings.

The important thing to note about credit union loans is that the interest rate is calculated on the *reducing balance* and is charged at a rate of *1% per month*. This makes credit unions the most competitive form of lending available. Your loan amount is also usually covered by loan protection insurance. In addition, because of the credit union structure, your original savings will remain with the credit union while you are paying off your loan. A point worth noting about credit union borrowing is that because of the pledge of secrecy which credit unions undertake in connection with their dealings with members, loans from the credit union are not part of the credit vetting system which is operated by the banks and building societies.

SUMMARY — BANKS AND CREDIT UNIONS

- Allways check the annual percentage rate, ie the true cost of borrowing, and select the lowest available.

- If possible, obtain term loans from the bank or credit union.
- The shorter the loan term, the less interest you will pay except with finance houses, where interest may be fixed. However, regular repayments will be higher on short term loans.
- Offer the minimum security required to obtain the cheapest lending rate.
- Get back your security when the loan is paid back, eg policies, share certs, deeds etc.
- Make sure that you are not spending too high a proportion of your income on debt, unless for a very good reason. Too high a debt/income proportion usually means spending has got out of control.
- Always examine whether you might be eligible for tax relief on loan interest. This could apply where the loan was obtained to buy a home or rental investment or for certain business purposes.

RENTING A HOME

In your twenties, you may consider the possibility of setting up your own home. There are two main options here: rent or buy. This chapter outlines some of the main points you need to consider if you intend to *rent* a property. Chapter 7 gives details you will need when you want to purchase.

BUDGETING

As always, the first question you should ask yourself is whether you can afford it. Examine your budget to see what your present spending is, and remember that you're going to be faced with greater costs than those you had perhaps experienced while living at home. New costs will include household bills, paying for your own transport, insurance, VHI, TV, etc. If there are any savings to be made, try to calculate these as well, eg travel, entertainment or whatever. Before you rent, have a good idea of *all* the costs involved and compare this with your present budget to see if it is affordable.

If you find it difficult to anticipate a likely budget picture, you could talk to somebody who is already renting to get some more information. If your budget picture looks very restricted, you might consider sharing to ease the financial burden.

Sharing

If you share your accommodation, this will naturally reduce your costs and it could perhaps make the transition less lonely for you. But there can be problems here as well. Will you get on with the people you share with? Who will manage the various household bills? Who will deal with the landlord? What happens to deposits/security if you leave the accommodation? If you are considering sharing, you would need to sort all these things out as early as possible. You may be thinking of sharing with a friend, and so you should be able to discuss these questions in some detail. If you are joining a group of strangers, this can be more awkward, but I would strongly recommend that all these questions are discussed in detail before you actually move in.

GENERAL CONDITIONS OF RENTING

Renting a property, whether a house or a flat, will usually be covered by a *lease*, which will set out the nature of the arrangement between yourself and your landlord. These leases may look rather daunting at first sight, as they are usually quite long and often contain a lot of legalistic language. You should, however, go through the conditions of the lease, as this is a *legally binding contract* between you and the landlord.

The main provisions usually cover:

(a) the rent;
(b) when rent is payable;
(c) the term of the lease, eg 6-12 months;
(d) any other costs that you have to pay, eg security, or heat;
(e) the responsibilities of the landlord, eg maintenance of certain items;
(f) your responsibilities regarding the property (what you must maintain);
(g) your responsibilities to other tenants, eg disturbance, parties, etc.

In certain instances, there may be no lease. This usually occurs when you are renting on a weekly basis. However, you should ask your landlord about the general arrangements covering the points mentioned already, as this verbal agreement between you forms the basis of your contract.

Expenses Involved

Apart from the cost of the rent itself, and your general household bills, there will be a number of initial expenses which you will have to meet. In the case of leasing arrangements, one month's rent may be payable in advance, together with a security deposit on the accommodation. You may also have to pay deposits for services such as the ESB. Accommodation will usually be let furnished, but if you've never lived away from home you will need things like linen, china, cutlery, pots, etc, which will be a once-off cost.

Security deposits are usually refunded when your lease is completed and are held as security by the landlord against damage to the accommodation. They can also be held against bills that might come in after you had vacated the accommodation.

Changing the Contract if you need to Vacate

When you are going to rent accommodation, it will usually

be your intention to stay there for at least a number of months. What happens if you find it necessary to leave your accommodation or find that you can't afford to pay the rent? You should look at the conditions with regard to giving notice, and let your landlord know as soon as possible when you will be vacating the apartment. If you have a lease for, say one year and have only been able to stay for six months, you could be required to pay rent for the outstanding term of the lease, but this is unusual. However, in that instance your security deposit would almost certainly be withheld.

SUMMARY

- Do a budget exercise before you rent to see if you can afford all the costs.
- Sources of accommodation information are newspapers, estate agents, friends and local newsagents.
- Consider sharing to ease the expense, and be sure to discuss all the financial arrangements before you move in.
- Examine any lease and agreement with a landlord carefully, as this is a legally binding contract.
- If you have to break a lease, give the landlord as much notice as possible.
- If you find you can't pay your rent, discuss the situation with your landlord and look for alternative accommodation, earlier rather than later.

SECTION 2 THE MIDDLE YEARS

BUYING A HOME

Because of tax relief, and also because of a strong history of home ownership, most people in Ireland buy their own home by the time they reach their mid-thirties. Before you undertake the purchase, there are a number of things you need to consider. The first of these is that it is usually necessary to have a least a *10% deposit* saved before you can proceed.

THE DEPOSIT

In my experience, many people have difficulty, not so much with their monthly mortgage repayments, particularly now since interest rates have fallen, but rather in accumulating the deposit which enables them to make the purchase. You have two options regarding this deposit: you can either save it or borrow it. However, many mortgage lenders do not like to see short-term loans for home deposits. This can be a mark against you in your mortgage application, unless your income is sufficient to carry both repayments.

MORTGAGE FINANCE

The main lenders on the mortgage market are the *building societies*, but the *banks* are taking a larger share all the time. Depending on your circumstances, you may also be entitled to a mortgage from your *local authority*, ie corporation or county council, and these loans are generally administered either by the housing finance agency or by the local authority.

In most mortgage applications there will be a number of costs involved such as an application fee, a survey fee, an indemnity bond where the mortgage is above 70% of the value of the property, the cost of insurance on the building, stamp duty on the mortgage and on the property in the case of a second-hand house, and legal fees. The advisors you will be dealing with during this purchase will be your solicitor, your financial advisor, your surveyor and perhaps an architect. If you have a financial advisor, she/he will usually complete the necessary paper work and liaise with your other advisors so that the purchase proceeds as smoothly as possible.

Costs Of Purchase

The types of costs that you may encounter depend on the lender that you choose, ie a building society, a bank or the local authority. However, some of the most common costs are as follows:

Application fee — this may be in the region of £50, and is charged by some building societies, and by the local authority;

Arrangement Fee — this can be a percentage of the mortgage amount payable on acceptance of the mortgage offer;

Valuation/Surveyor's fee — certain of the banks may allow you to use your own surveyor without having to pay for a surveyor for the bank as well. Typical surveyor's fees will vary from £50 to £100 as a maximum, plus mileage and VAT.

Indemnity Bond — this is quite common amongst the building societies where the amount of the mortgage exceeds 70% of the value of the property. This is a once-off charge and is a percentage of the difference between 70% and the size of the mortgage. Some of the building societies may add this to your mortgage — for example, on a mortgage of £40,500 which is 90% of the purchase price, a bond on £9,000 would be required, costing approximately £270.

Buildings Insurance — you will need to insure the building for the full re-instatement value as part of the security necessary to complete the transaction. You should effect this insurance from the date contracts are exchanged. The lender will tell you the value that they wish the building to be insured for. An average rate of building insurance would be £1.60 per thousand, so a £40,000 house would cost £64 pa and government duty.

Completion of the Mortgage Deed — although building society legislation was changed so that building societies could no longer charge legal fees in connection with mortgages, in practice many continue to do so under the above heading. This is what is known as costs attaching to completion or drawing up the mortgage deed, and can vary quite substantially from lender to lender. Some may charge nothing or as little as £70, whereas others may charge much more. Be sure to check as far as possible exactly how much this charge may be.

Legal Fees — you will need a solicitor to complete the transfer of ownership of property to yourself. There are some general guidelines as to what solicitors can charge for these transactions. A fairly common charge is 1% of the price plus £100 for professional services. VAT is payable at 25% on professional fees.

You will also have to pay charges for having the property registered in your name either in the Land Registry or in the Registry of Deeds. Land Registry charges range from £50 to £200, where the purchase price exceeds £30,000. In the Registry of Deeds the charge is £20.

Stamp Duty on Second-Hand Property — This tax is payable on second-hand houses on completion of the transaction. The current rates are:

IR£'s	
10,001-20,000	3%
20,001-50,000	4%
50,001-60,000	5%
60,001 plus	6%

Stamp duty is payable on the building rather than any of the contents, so where you have bought a second-hand property to include furnishings, there should be some reduction on the overall price for the purposes of calculating stamp duty.

There is also a stamp duty of 25p per £200 for mortgages over £10,000. This duty is payable on the *full* amount.

Lending Requirements of the Different Lending Institutions

The two main players in this market are the banks and the building societies. Building societies have a preference for lending to savers, although this is becoming less the case of late because of increased competition. However, although you may not be required to have savings with the building society, do check whether you are being charged a different interest rate because of the fact that you have not had savings with the society for a particular period of time. There can sometimes be a loading on interest rates of between ½% and 1%. Generally, some of the building societies' initial costs may be higher than some of the banks, although they do have a slight edge on the banks in terms of the interest rate on the mortgage itself. Almost all banks and building societies now offer endowment mortgages as well as repayment mortgages. A point to watch is whether you are offered a choice of endowment company with any particular bank or building society. There can be differences in the conditions on different endowment policies and also in the performance records of different endowment companies. It can be to your advantage if there is some choice of endowment company, should you decide to go the endowment route.

Lenders will offer between 90-95% of the purchase price of the property or some multiple of salary/salaries (eg two and a half to three times main and one time smaller, whichever is the lesser.)

Ideally what you should be looking for in your mortgage is to obtain the cheapest interest rate available to you and the lowest initial costs, together with the availability of a choice of insurance company.

Local Authority Loans

County council or corporation loans can be a source of mortgage finance for certain types of purchasers.

Between £21,000 and £22,500 may be available from the local authority, where your income has not exceeded £10,000 in the previous tax year, and where you have been refused a mortgage by a bank or building society.

For single parents, and people who have been in or are waiting for local housing, the mortgage amount may be extended to £27,000. Income limits do not apply to these special category loans.

Interest on loans from the local authority can either be at a variable rate or linked to the present rate of inflation. Variable interest rates at the moment are 8.47% and those that are fixed to the inflation rate charge 5.75% above the consumer price index.

Mortgage types available from the local authority are:

1 Annuity loans, where interest and capital is paid off through the mortgage term;
2 Income related loans, where repayments are based on income for the previous tax year, but may never fall below 90% of the repayment for the previous year;
3 Convertible loans, where repayments are linked to income for the first five years, then convert to the annuity method.

If your income is below £10,000 per annum you should consider applying to the local authority for a mortgage. Interest rates in general tend to be quite competitive with the building societies, and in fact income-related loans have recently had a lower interest rate than those available elsewhere in the market. With income-related loans, however, you should ensure that you always pay at least the interest each year, so that the principal outstanding does not increase.

Bank/Building Society Mortgages

The main types of mortgage you will meet will be the *repayment, or annuity mortgage*, as already described, and the *endowment mortgage*, where interest only is paid to the lender and an endowment policy is undertaken, which builds up the capital sum to repay the loan at the end of the term.

Endowment Mortgages Versus Annuity Mortgages — An endowment mortgage, as well as paying your loan, *is a way of saving*. The aim is that, in addition to paying off the original loan amount, there would be a surplus in the policy at the end of the term, which would be available to the policy holder as a tax-free lump sum. The attractiveness to you of the annuity or endowment method depends on your tax position and savings requirement. If you compare the net repayments on the capital and interest method and the endowment method, many higher rate tax-payers and couples find only slight differences between the two. In general, over a 20-year term, the endowment method will usually end up costing less than the repayment method.

Although the endowment mortgage will generally be more attractive, there are certain instances where the repayment mortgage may make more sense. This might be the case where a shorter mortgage term is involved, ie 5-10 years; where you intend to leave the country within a few years; or, in the instance of an older person, where the endowment premiums might be quite expensive. You should consider your own situation, comparing gross and net repayments now and in the future, and in this way you will be able to see which is more to your advantage.

Types of Endowment Mortgages — If the endowment method is the route you have decided on, you may find when you approach the lender that two types of endowment are offered to you, with significantly different premiums. One of these will undoubtedly be what is known as a *full cost endowment*, ie the one with the higher premiums, and the other will be a *low cost endowment*. A full cost endowment is when you save more than the minimum requirement to pay off the loan amount at the end of the mortgage term. This is with the idea of producing a much larger capital sum for yourself, as well as paying off the loan amount. The low cost endowment mortgage, by comparison, gears the premiums so that they will produce the loan amount and perhaps some surplus, rather than a significant amount in excess of the loan. Endowment policies can operate on a unit linked basis or a with-profit basis and depending on your attitude to risk, your age and the mortgage term, you may choose one or other of these approaches.

BUYING YOUR HOME

The first step is to obtain either a generalised mortgage approval certificate from the lender of your choice (these are available from certain of the banks and some of the building societies) or alternatively to find a property, after which you make your mortgage application. When you make your mortgage application, you should evaluate whether the endowment or repayment method is more suitable for you and then undertake all the necessary paperwork. *Before you pay any money for your property, be sure to consult your solicitor* so that any conditions necessary for the repayment of monies to you are written into your offer on the property. For new houses, there can sometimes be a booking deposit of £100 and this can be in addition to the normal 10% deposit, or inclusive.

On receipt of contracts, you will be required to pay your 10% deposit, usually subject to mortgage approval, satisfactory title and planning. In the case of a new building, it is also subject to the satisfactory completion of the property. When you have exchanged contracts, you arrange a completion date, say four to six weeks later. This is usually sufficient to enable your solicitor to undertake the necessary searches, etc, that she/he may find necessary. In the case of a new property, as well as the first survey, a final survey may be necessary. With building societies this will cost you a further £40 approximately.

When everything is organised to *your own and your solicitor's satisfaction*, you finalise your closing date. At closing, you will need your mortgage protection or endowment policy as security for the lender. You will also need to have undertaken building insurance. Normally, this should be arranged at exchange of contracts (check this point with your solicitor). These policies and insurances are the security on which the mortgage is being offered and without them the lender will usually not release the mortgage cheque. At closing, you will have to pay any stamp duty that you are liable for and if your mortgage amount is less than 90% you will also have to pay any balance due to the vendor or builder.

Bridging Finance

This used to be the dread of most borrowers and until recently it was quite common. Now, however, it is less often necessary and is to be avoided if at all possible. This is because the interest rate for bridging finance is quite a bit higher than that available for mortgage finance. It therefore costs you more money. However, there are certan situations where it may be necessary, for example if you are building your own house and mortgage finance is not available until the property is fully completed. Alternatively, you may be in the process of selling your own house and buying another and need to complete the new purchase before you can complete your own sale. If you are paying interest on two properties, bridging finance may be allowed for tax purposes, as well as your mortgage interest. Details of all the interest should be submitted with your tax returns to see whether you are entitled to relief.

How To Claim Tax Relief

After completion, you should receive from the lender a certificate of estimated interest either to the calendar year end or to the subsequent 5 April, and you should immediately forward this to your Inspector of Taxes. In addition, you should send your *life assurance premium relief certificates* to your Inspector of Taxes, as this is the second heading under which you will be entitled to tax relief following your property purchase. It is now standard for the Revenue Commissioners to issue you with a form requesting details as to how you provided the finance for this property purchase. This will request details of the amount of money that you provided yourself, any money that was provided by way of gift or loan, and, in the case of savings, it will also request deposit interest certificates for the past five years. If you have been completing tax returns, you will most likely have given details of these savings for previous years. If you have not been completing tax returns, most probably because you are in PAYE employment, you will now have to give details of your savings. PAYE earners receive tax relief immediately in their net salary, whereas for those who are self-employed tax relief is available by way of a reduction in their potential tax liability at the year end.

ONGOING COSTS OF PROPERTY

Property ownership will involve you in regular costs each year, and it is as well to have some idea of what to expect. If the property is new, the initial decoration and furniture will probably be sufficient to last for a number of years. However, every year you will have to pay for *building insurance*. Some people may also have to pay *property tax*. For those who purchase apartments, there is usually an *annual service charge*, and even with a new property it is a good idea to budget for a certain amount of *maintenance costs* each year.

Return on Investment?

In calculating the return on investment that one is likely to get on property, people are inclined to forget these ongoing costs and simply deduct the initial price from their subsequent sale price to see what profit they have made. This is not a true calculation of your real rate of return. You must include the costs of the original purchase, ie fees, stamp duty, etc, as well as all costs between the original purchase and the subsequent sale, ie maintenance, charges, etc, and only then can you really see your return on investment. Since the property is also acting as your home, this element (ie rent cost) needs to be included. However, return on investment is perhaps not your main concern. Nevertheless, you should keep it in mind. Property purchased in good locations should offer reasonable returns in the medium- to long-term.

SUMMARY

- Try to plan to buy, allowing yourself one year to save your 10% deposit and costs.
- If you have no deposit, see if you can obtain a personal loan from a relative, or a term loan from the credit union.
- Remember, mortgage lenders prefer you to have no other borrowing if possible. However, if your income is good, you may be able to obtain 100% finance in a mortgage/term loan combination.
- Study all the costs and interest rates of the different lenders and try to get the lowest interest rate and initial expenses possible, consistent with your loan requirement.
- Look carefully at the tax implications of different mortgage types — for 48% to 56% taxpayers, the endowment method is more tax efficient.
- Never pay money to either a builder or a seller without first consulting your solicitor.
- To ensure that you receive tax relief as soon as possible, it is a good idea to have your tax affairs up to date. When you buy a house, the Revenue Commissioners will ask how you financed the purchase.
- Review your budgeting arrangements following property purchase and include new costs, such as insurance, maintenance, etc, in your revised budget picture.

SOME THOUGHTS ON MARRIAGE

When people are getting married, finances (other than the cost of the wedding, honeymoon or house deposit) are often the farthest things from their mind. Equally, the 'romance' of the occasion can make people wish to avoid the subject of money, as they feel that their thoughts should be on higher (or other) things! However, some attention should be paid to the question of cash and asset management and the following are some thoughts on the major areas which will require consideration.

BEFORE MARRIAGE

You may operate jointly or separately before marriage. Usually your personal finances will be kept separate, eg rent, clothing, etc, (where you are not living together) but often people save together to buy a home in the future. Where this sort of 'joint' savings is undertaken, be sure that the account is in your joint names, even if you are not contributing the same amount each week or month. This is essential to ensure that in the event of anything happening to either of you, or in the event of some dispute, the money can be withdrawn and split between you. Joint accounts mean that both parties hold equal shares, although in fact the contributions may not be equal. However, 'joint' has legal implications and it can be useful to start becoming familiar with these before you actually 'tie the knot'.

Once you have started saving jointly, and have definite plans to marry, you should address the question of joint budgeting after marriage. This basically means how you would intend to split the bills and would often be according to the means of the two parties. However, every couple is different and the point is to discuss the matter beforehand and not make any assumptions.

Where couples are engaged, certain legal provisions contained in the Family Law Act 1981 govern joint property in the event of a disagreement, but for other couples there would have to be some agreement on how joint assets would be split in the event of a relationship breaking up.

It can happen that one or other of the couple will have

already bought a house, usually in their sole name. Before marriage, some thought would need to be given as to how this asset would be dealt with after marriage, ie would it be sold and the proceeds used to purchase a joint property? Would it be retained and rented? or, would it be put into joint names and become the family home? Where it is retained in the original sole name, ownership of the asset is clear-cut. However, where it is to be put into joint names, the question arises as to how much the original party contributed towards the purchase of the asset, and you would need to discuss whether any contribution was now going to be made by the person acquiring joint ownership to even-out the investment. This decision is obviously up to the people involved. However, for tax reasons, if you are going to transfer a single property into joint ownership, it is wise to wait until after the marriage.

ON MARRIAGE

Your legal status changes on marriage and you will now both have responsibilities towards each other, legal and financial, and towards any children that you already have, or may have in the future. Both people can continue to hold assets in their single names and you will probably also acquire assets which will be owned jointly. Where an asset is held jointly, ownership is 50/50. To avoid future complications, it would now be very wise to ensure that the family home is in joint names and this can be done with the minimum of legal and tax costs.

Marriage and Tax

The income of a married woman who is living with her husband is automatically regarded as her husband's income for tax purposes, unless either spouse gives written notice to the Inspector before the end of the tax year that she/he wishes to be taxed separately. It seldom makes financial sense for couples to be taxed as single persons, but *it is up to you both to decide how the tax allowances should be divided.* If one of you is self-employed and the other in PAYE employment, it can make sense, cash flow-wise, to give all the allowances to the PAYE person. However, this means that the self-employed partner will pay tax on all profits earned, without the benefit of any allowance. To decide how to divide the allowances fairly, you need to look at the net income of both partners, with and without allowances, and put this into the context of your agreed joint budget.

Budgeting after Marriage

As you will now be jointly responsibe for your various bills. It makes sense to review your budget picture and set up some system to deal with this joint expenditure. It can be a good idea to open a joint account for bills, etc. and to decide how much each partner will contribute. It is not necessary to have all your income going into this account, and it may not be desirable. For personal spending, a single account is more appropriate. Every couple will devise their own system of managing their joint income but it is important to realise that the one who pays for all the day-to-day necessities such as shopping, entertainment, etc, is contributing just as vital a share to the joint budget as the partner who pays the bills.

SOME LONGER TERM CONSIDERATIONS

When a person marries, if they have already made a will this now becomes invalid, unless it was made with the marriage in mind. You should therefore review any previous wills, and it is always a good idea to look at this question and draw up a will, expressing your wishes clearly in the event of your death. The necessary steps to do this are dealt with in Chapter 9. You should now also consider what might happen to your partner in the event of your death, and decide whether you wish to protect against this eventuality. Again, how to undertake this protection is outlined in Chapter 9. In time, you may have children and one of you may undertake to look after them full-time. In that case, one income would cease, and this would be a time to review joint finances again. Children are a joint decision and where one party cares for them full-time, this should not have the effect of diminishing her/his financial independance, except in so far as it reduces the overall family income through a loss of earnings. Income that might be transferred from one partner to the other should be on a formalised basis, eg by standing order to a personal account. This ensures that the homemaker has charge of her/his own income.

SUMMARY

- Marriage is a very personal matter but financial matters are involved in it at all stages.
- The implications for tax, budgeting and legal owernship of assets should be considered before marriage and should be reviewed on a regular basis.

THE PROTECTION RACKET — INSURING AGAINST RISKS

Before looking at how best to provide for protection, you need to understand the types of risk that you are likely to face.

Risks that should be considered are those of death, short- or long-term illness, the risk of hospitalisation and the risk to one's property, eg house, contents, car, etc. Obviously, you hope to be able to avoid most of these eventualities, but in the case of *death*, it is *not a matter of 'if' but rather of 'when'*. Even if the probability is that a number of these risks will not occur, it is sensible to consider protecting against them and to know what cover is available.

LIFE ASSURANCE

You can insure your own life so that cash will be paid if your death occurs, in certain circumstances. The circumstances can be that (a) a payment will occur on your death at any age, or (b) a payment will occur on your death within a specified period. Both options come under the heading of life assurance.

Option A — Risk and Savings

Option A is generally known as *'whole of life cover'*. Because of the certainty of death, this option can be reasonably expensive to insure against, depending on your age and health. It will certainly be more expensive than insuring against Option B, as there is an element of savings in the premium on a 'whole of life policy'. This means that after a certain number of years the policy will acquire an *encashment value*, provided a reasonable rather than a very high level of life assurance is chosen at the start of the policy. This type of life assurance can produce a reasonable return on investment in the medium to long-term and can be used to provide cash rather than a death benefit, should you so wish.

Option B — Risk Cover Only

Option B, ie the payment of a benefit on death within a specified period, has no element of savings at all and the premiums which are paid are used to *cover the risk element only*. The higher the risk, the higher the premium, but because cover will cease at a specified time in the future, there is a good possibility that the company will not have to make any payment. Because of these two factors, this type of risk cover can be quite cheap to buy and is usually the first type of protection to be considered. Option B can be arranged in three ways:

1. **Level Term Assurance** — this is where the sum assured and the time period are selected at the outset (eg £50,000 for 20 years), and depending on the age and state of health of the applicant, premiums are set at the beginning and will not vary over the term selected.
2. **Convertible Term Assurance** — this is a variation of term assurance but builds in an *option* at the beginning to convert the policy at any stage during the term to a 'whole of life policy', ie one that will pay out on death whenever it occurs, *without any further medical evidence*. This last point relating to medical evidence is what makes the conversion option valuable.
3. **Decreasing Term Assurance** — this type of insurance is most familiar in the form of mortgage protection for the traditional repayment mortgage, where the capital outstanding reduces over the lifetime of the mortgage and so does the sum insured on the mortgage protection policy. Initially premiums will be fixed in relation to the interest rate, but because no one knows future rates, premiums will usually cover a range of interest rates around the actual rate at the time of assuming the risk.

Family and Income Assurance

A fourth variation of life assurance is to have the sum assured paid out by way of a regular income after the death of the person insured. This payment lasts for a specified amount of time and is paid to the nominated beneficiary of the policy. This type of cover is usually called a *family income policy*. However, it is similar to other forms of life assurance in that it is 'Risk Cover Only'.

Which to Choose?

The type of insurance you choose will depend on your situation and on how best your beneficiaries might be able to use the sum assured. Generally speaking, as long as the proceeds of life assurance remain tax-free, a beneficiary usually has more options by receiving the full sum assured rather than by receiving it spread out over a period of time.

Making a Will

Thinking about the question of death leads naturally to the question of what you would like to happen to your assets, in the event of death. Often people assume that either they have very few assets, or very straightforward family dependants, and therefore have no need to make a will. Even if there are very few assets or dependants, making a will makes the whole procedure in the event of death very much easier. This can mean less hardship and difficulty for those left behind and usually shortens the time taken to wind up the deceased's estate. This also saves on costs such as legal fees. Therefore, I strongly recommend everyone to *make a will.* It is, in fact, vital where you wish to leave assets to people outside the family, as these people have no rights under the laws of succession.

Succession Rights

When people are married, it is usually not possible to disinherit a spouse. Even where there is a will disinheriting a spouse, a surviving spouse has a *legal minimum right* to *one half* of the deceased's estate, where there are no children, or *one-third* of the estate, where there are children. In cases of separation or desertion, these rights may alter, but even where succession has been waived by partners to a separation, or has been lost through desertion, a will is vitally important. Succession rights are open to legal interpretation and unless there are specific instructions a person's estate may come, by default, to a separated spouse, at least in part.

The whole subject of death and wills is, naturally, an emotional one and unfortunately many people tend to ignore it. The main point to ensure when making a will is that *whatever assets arise from your death are given to the people of your choice.* Otherwise, the decision passes into the law with only your family, or ultimately the state, being entitled to benefit.

Table 3 outlines the laws of succession where there is no will. Where there is a will (unless you are married) you really can decide to leave your estate to anyone, for example a charity or an unrelated person. Remember, the decision is yours.

TABLE 3 — WHEN THERE IS A WILL

Surviving Relatives:	Distribution of Estate where deceased dies intestate.
Spouse and Children:	Two-thirds to spouse, one-third to children in equal shares. Children of deceased son or daughter get their parent's share.
Children, no spouse:	Whole estate to children in equal shares. Children of a deceased son or daughter get their parent's share.
Father, Mother, Brothers, Sisters:	One-half to each parent.
Parent, Brothers and Sisters:	Whole estate to parent.
Brothers and Sisters:	All get equal shares with children of deceased brothers and sisters getting their parent's share.
Nephews and Nieces:	All get equal shares.
Remoter next-of-kin:	All get equal shares.

Steps in Making a Will

So, how do you go about making a will? The first step is to list all your *assets* eg house, savings, life assurance, pension, investments, etc. You should then also list all your *liabilities*. This will enable you to see what your net worth is. Having done this, you should decide whom you would like to *benefit* in the event of your death — usually you should express this in percentage terms in relation to the full value of your estate, or a particular item, for instance, your house. You should also make a provision for any *residue* of the estate, after specific bequests, for where part of your assets are bequeathed to someone, but the residue is not, this omission invalidates the will. You will need to select those whom you would like to *administer the estate*; these will usually be people whom you trust to carry out your wishes. You should also feel that they would handle the matter efficiently, and at a reasonable cost. These people (called the executor/s) can benefit under the estate. This is a responsible and sometimes difficult task, and it is usually a good idea to have more than one executor. Finally, you need to have your will *witnessed* by two people; *these cannot be beneficiaries.* Remember that they do not need to know the content of the will, simply witness your signature.

It is not essential to have legal advice for a will to be effective. However, as a will is final and very important, it is certainly useful to obtain professional advice.

A final point regarding inheritance is that beneficiaries may or may not be liable to tax. In Ireland, this situation is made more difficult by the fact that there is no divorce and therefore partners in a second union may be 'unrelated' to each other, as far as tax purposes are concerned. In the event of receiving a bequest under a will, you may be subject to capital acquisitions tax. Table 4 lists the tax thresholds for capital acquisitions tax and the rates of tax effective once these thresholds are passed. It is possible to give benefits to people while you are still alive, and these benefits will also be assessed as far as tax is concerned. However, these are seen as gifts and the rate of tax effective on these gifts will be only 75% of the rate of tax applying if these benefits had passed to the people concerned on your death.

TABLE 4 — CAPITAL ACQUISITIONS TAX, BENEFITING PERSONS, AMOUNT OF TAX-FREE BENEFIT AND RATES OF APPLICABLE TAX THEREAFTER

BENEFITING PERSON	AMOUNT OF TAX FREE CASH
Husband or Wife	No Limit
Children	£150,000
Brothers/Sisters Niece/Nephews	£20,000
No relationship	£10,000
Deserving nieces or nephews (treated as with children)	£150,000
Rates of tax on amounts received above the tax-free amounts	
Next £10,000	20%
Next £40,000	30%
Next £50,000	35%
Next £50,000	40%
Next £50,000	45%
Balance	55%

PROTECTION AGAINST ILLNESS

The risk of illness, either short — or long-term, is much higher than the risk of death before age 65, so it makes sense to consider what would happen to you if this situation arises. You will usually be trying to cover two aspects, ie that you will continue to receive an income while ill, and that any expenses which arise from your illness will be provided for.

Income Protection

Illness of a short-term nature will usually be covered, in income terms, by either one's employment, by social insurance contributions or by some combination of these two. You should always check with your employer regarding your pay entitlements if you are sick for more than a few days. Some employers may continue to pay you in full for up to six months, while others may not. Where you are not protected by your employer, you need to apply to social welfare for disability benefit and to receive this you must satisfy the following conditions:

1. You must be unfit for work due to illness;
2. You must have at least 39 weeks PRSI paid and 39 weeks paid or credited in the governing tax year. To get benefit at the full rate, 48 weeks PRSI paid or credit are needed in the governing year;
3. You must be under 66.

Disability benefit can continue for as long as you are unable to work, and under age 66 if you have a total of 260 PRSI contributions paid since starting work. If you have less than this number, disability benefit can be paid for up to 52 weeks. At the end of this period, you can requalify for benefit by working and paying PRSI for a further 13 weeks (or a smaller number if it brings your total to 260).

This benefit can also involve some pay-related income; again this will depend on your contributions and level of income. Pay-related benefit will not normally be paid for the first three weeks but may then continue for 375 days.

If you continue to be unwell after one year, and do not satisfy the PRSI conditions for continuing disability benefit, you should check with the Department of Social Welfare to see whether you would be entitled to any other form of payment. Check also with your health board to see whether you would be entitled to a maintenance allowance (A companion handbook, **Social Welfare For Women,** gives fuller details on this type of income).

It is not difficult to see that if you are dependent on social insurance alone to protect your income in the event of illness, a severe drop in income could be the likely long-term result. To supplement social welfare cover, it is possible to *insure oneself for a loss of income* and your employment may offer this type of cover as part of your pension scheme — usually termed income continuance benefit.

Income Continuance or Permanent Health Insurance is an insurance which is designed to provide you with a portion of your previous income, should you be ill for an extended period. Once a claim is made, the payment will continue until you go back to work or until retirement age, whichever is the sooner. One claim does not disqualify you from future claims — this is the meaning of the word permanent in the title — and the cover cannot usually be withdrawn by the insurance company, except in the case of fraud. At first glance, this type of cover seems ideal for anyone wishing to protect their income and indeed it is, providing you understand how it works. There are a number of important conditions which must be remembered, the most important being that you cannot earn more while sick than you did while working; this restriction is laid down by the Revenue Commissioners. Your total income may not exceed two-thirds of your previous pay. Income paid out from this type of insurance will be treated, for tax purposes, in the same way as your previous income from employment and can commence after 13 weeks' illness.

A final important point about this type of insurance relates to how 'disability' is defined. The cover provided by the insurance may be for loss of income from any or all employments rather than your usual employment. Basically, this means that payment will occur only if you cannot work at all, because of illness or accident. Remember that this will have to be medically verified, and if the claim is long-term, medical attendant's reports will have to be sent to the insurance company on a regular basis. Be sure to check how 'disability' is defined when undertaking this type of cover.

Hospital Income Plans/Accident Policies

An interim and shorter-term type of income protection is also provided by some accident policies and by hospital income plans. These may pay out a certain amount of regular money, eg £25 — £40 — £60 per day, or £100 per week, for a limited period, the maximum period being usually one year. However, the definition in the insurance is quite specific, ie accident means just that and does not cover illness not caused by an accident and hospital income usually means that the income will be paid while in hospital only, due to accident or illness. Payment can start without any great waiting period and as these policies are inexpensive, eg £4 to £10 per month, they can provide a useful temporary type of income cover.

Protection Against Expenses Arising From Illness

Voluntary Health Insurance (VHI) As well as trying to secure regular income for yourself in the event of illness, you may be concerned to insure against expenses that would arise if you were hospitalised or had significant ongoing medical expenses. The Voluntary Health Insurance Board (VHI) is the only health insurer in Ireland and offers a wide range of plans to cover expenses of different types of hospital and treatment care. There are currently five plans to choose from — A, B, C, D and E. Each plan provides cover for a different level of maintenance as well as an annual benefit for eligible outpatient expenses.

In addition to covering hospital costs, each plan includes cover for a number of outpatient expenses over a certain amount, subject to certain limits. The first £170 for a family, or £105 for an individual, is not covered and the maximum benefits are £1,000 for Plan A, £1,200 for Plan B, and £1,400 for Plans C, D and E. Eligible outpatient expenses are:

- general practitioners' fees;
- consultants' fees;
- prescribed drugs (this type of cover is currently being reviewed and will probably be withdrawn in the near future);
- doctors' fees for pre- and post-natal care;
- physiotherapy (necessary because of accident or illness);
- home nursing, when certified as essential for medical reasons (maximum of £15 a day for 42 days in any subscription year);
- medical and surgical appliances as specified by the VHI;
- emergency dental treatment arising from an accident; public hospital outpatient and casualty charges.

Benefit for professional fees, is also provided by way of *fee units.* It is not guaranteed to cover the full fees, but by purchasing the recommended number of fee units you should provide a realistic level of protection for typical charges.

If you are not a member of the VHI you are, of course, entitled to free medical care in a public ward of a public hospital. However, this care may be allocated on the basis of need and the care is paid for by the state, whose resources for health care are presently being reduced. You could find yourself waiting for a considerable length of time for any care or treatment of a non-critical nature.

PROTECTION OF YOUR PROPERTY

As well as life and sickness cover, you will also need to consider whether you wish to guard against the risk of damage or loss to your property. The most common forms of property insurance are those for cars, buildings, contents and valuable items in general. Certain types of basic property insurance are required by law, eg if you own a car, you must insure it, and if you buy a house with a mortgage the lender will usually insist that the property is insured for its full reinstatement value.

Car Insurance

Check which type of cover is appropriate to the car and its drivers. Shop around, as costs are highly competitive, and look for special deals now being offered to women.

Property Insurance

In regard to insuring your buildings, ie your house or apartment, it can be a condition of your loan that the property is insured for the full reinstatement value. This is not the market value or the price that you would expect to sell your property for, but rather the cost of rebuilding the property from scratch, to include clearing off the site, fees, etc. However for older properties, where there may be no mortgage, building insurance may be more linked in the owner's mind to the sale value of the property. This is not always the best level of cover and in the event of a claim you could find that the payment you received was subject to an averaging clause.

The Averaging Clause A situation where averaging might apply would be where you had a sum insured on your property in total of, say, £30,000, which you had assumed was close to the market value of your house. Your home is damaged by fire and you wish to make a claim of £15,000. On receipt of the claim, the insurance company assesses the cost of rebuilding the house as new. If they assess this as being higher than the cover that you paid for, they only pay you a proportion of the figure that you have claimed, this being calculated as the proportion of the sum insured over the assessed total rebuilding costs. You could therefore find yourself having to meet quite a lot of the refurbishment costs out of your own pocket. When insuring buildings it is necessary to be realistic as to the full cost of reinstatement. Also be aware of what is, and is not, covered.

Contents Contents insurance relates to items of furniture and fittings, together with items like curtains, carpets, etc. This insurance will cover the cost of replacing contents in the event of fire, theft, flood, etc, ie standard perils, and items covered in this way are usually in your house at all times. Cover can either be on a *new for old basis* or on what is known as an *indemnity basis* — this means that you only receive the amount that the insurance company assessed the item was actually worth at the time of the damage. Buildings insurance would usually cover fixed fittings in your house, eg fitted wardrobes, presses, and may cover outside fixtures such as fences, but be sure to check your particular policy.

All-risks or accidental damage cover is most appropriate to items of jewellery or other valuables which can be in your home but which might also be moved outside. This cover protects these items from the usual risks, eg fire, theft, but will also protect against loss as a result of your own carelessness.

Optional extras which may be included in your buildings or contents insurance policy are cover for items such as sports equipment, pedal cycles, personal money and credit cards, caravans, camping equipment, and fridge-freezer contents. There will usually be an extra charge for this type of cover but you should always look at your own situation and see if it is applicable.

A final point regarding property insurance is that some companies now offer *no claims bonuses* and *discounts* on buildings/contents insurance; this can in some way reduce the cost of your premium; if you have not had a claim for some time. A discount might be available for burglar or smoke alarms and this will usually involve a reduction in your premium by some percentage. It is also becoming more common for premiums to be paid throughout the year rather than in a single sum. This can be useful in spreading the cost and there is usually a small charge for this type of policy.

SUMMARY

- Where money is tight, insurance is often seen as a luxury. However, you only have to read the papers or listen to the news to see all the people for whom potential 'risks' have become reality.
- Any comprehensive look at your protection requirements should therefore certainly examine the major risk possibilities and even if you can't protect against them all, try to assess which ones you would be most concerned

about and start with covering them. What you are looking for is to protect against the risk in a comprehensive way, and at a reasonable price.

- Always understand what is, and is not, covered, and the events that are necessary for the cover to be effective.
- Look out for special deals and try to ease the financial burden of the insurance by setting it up automatically on direct debit or standing order and if possible spread over the full year rather than in a single sum.
- If you have a taxable income, check if the insurance is eligible for tax relief, eg VHI, Permanent Health Insurance, and claim whatever relief is available, so reducing the true cost to you.
- Make a will, as this ensures that your wishes will be carried out and it will make things much easier for those left behind.

HOW TO MAXIMISE YOUR TAX RELIEF

As everyone knows, our income tax rates are very high. It therefore makes sense to avail of any reliefs that are available to you, whether you are paying tax on the PAYE system or through self-employed assessment. Unless you claim reliefs due to you you will be paying more tax than necessary, (although it is possible to claim tax relief retrospectively over a number of years). However, if you have a good general understanding of the system, you should be able to get the tax relief due to you each year. Always remember that any change in your financial arrangements should be reviewed in the light of their tax implications and any new tax relief claimed. In my experience, there are many people who never claim allowances to which they are entitled, for example life assurance premium relief, VHI, etc. The important thing to remember is that it is your money, and if you don't see that the figures are right, no -one else is likely to.

PAYE EMPLOYEES

For employees, the first thing you should check is your certificate of tax-free allowances. Make sure, firstly, that you are getting your basic allowances, and secondly that you are on the correct table. The basic tax-free allowances that everyone is entitled to are (1) your personal allowance; £2,050 for a single person, £2,550 for a widowed person and £4,100 for a married couple; (2) PAYE allowance of £800, if you are taxed under PAYE; (3) a PRSI allowance of £286, if you pay any of the higher rates of PRSI. To see which tax table you should be on, you should add all your allowances to the tax bands and see whether your income falls into either the 32%, 48% or 56% bracket. Then check your tax-free allowance to see that you are getting the appropriate tax table allowance, as well as your normal basic allowances. The size of the tax-free allowances and the bands will vary depending on whether you are single or married. If you are married and you both work outside the home, the two incomes need to be added together to get the total of your taxable income. Deduct your basic allowances and the balance will indicate the appropriate tax band.

Case 1

Mary is single and her gross salary is £12,000. She lives at home, has no mortgage and no other income apart from her salary. She pays A1 rate PRSI. Her tax payable calculation is as follows:

Total Income	£12,000
Less Personal Allowance	£2,050
PAYE Allowance	£800
PRSI Allowance	£286
Taxable Income	£8,864
Table A Band	£6,100 at 32%
Balance — all within B Band	£2,764 at 48%

Mary's income therefore places her on tax table B and this would mean that all her income throughout the year would be taxed at 48%. To even out her income pattern, she should ensure that she has a table 'B' allowance of £2034 pa.

Case 2

Bernadette and Tom are married and have two salaries. Bernadette earns £12,000, Tom earns £16,000, total £28,000. They have a mortgage of £28,000 and pay annual VHI premiums of £350 plus life assurance premiums of £240. They have no other income and both pay A1 PRSI. Their tax calculation is as follows:

Total Income	£28,000
Less Personal Allowance	£4,100
PAYE Allowance (X by 2)	£1,600
PRSI Allowance (X by 2)	£572
Mortgage Interest Relief (90% of £28,000 x 8.25%)	£2,079
VHI (allowed in full)	£350
Life Assurance (ie half the annual premiums)	£120
Taxable Income	£19,179
Tax Table R	£12,200 at 32%
Balance	£6,979
Tax Table	£6,200 at 48%
Balance	£779 at 56%

Bernadette and Tom are edging into the 56% tax bracket and should either be on table R or table S. An important point to remember in Ireland, given our divorce situation, is that to avail of married tax allowances and bands you must be legally married.

In both these examples, the taxpayers should check to see that they have the proper tax table allowance. The purpose of this extra allowance is to offset the higher starting rate of tax paid and to even out the total tax paid throughout the year. If you are on the wrong table, you should not end up paying more tax over the full year, but you will pay more of your tax towards the year end, so your net salary will vary, ie it will decrease as the year goes on. It makes sense, therefore, to be on the right table, and where your income is fixed you can easily calculate what your highest tax rate will be. Table allowances do not apply to self-employed people, although the tax bands for taxable income are the same. Self-employed persons pay their tax in one lump sum, so for them the table allowance is irrelevant.

If you do not agree with the calculation of your total tax liability, be sure to ask for a balancing statement which shows how your Inspector of Taxes made the calculation.

Allowances

The most common allowances against tax are the following:
Mortgage Interest Relief — you are allowed relief on interest paid in respect of a main private residence mortgage up to 80% of £2,000 per annum (single person) ie £1,600 per annum, or 80% of £4,000 per annum (married persons) ie £3,200, or 80% of £2,900 per annum (widowed person) ie £2,320 per annum. These overall maximums usually relate to your main private residence but can include interest paid for bridging for a limit period, and interest paid in respect of the home of a separated spouse.

If you want to maximise mortgage interest, you could consider converting your repayment mortgage to an endowment mortgage, if you still have a good proportion of the term of the mortgage to run.

Pension Investment — a pension investment is essential to provide for old age and it does not do to rely solely on the possibility of a state pension. Where additional provision is made by the taxpayer over and above PRSI, the state contributes generously by way of tax relief. All pension contributions up to a maximum of 15% of earnings are fully deductible for tax purposes. This means that £1 invested only costs between 68p and 44p. Pensions, and how to go about arranging them, will be discussed in more detail in Chapter 12.

Life Assurance Premium Relief — relief is available on 40% of the premiums paid to any policies which insure the life of the taxpayer or her/his spouse. The maximum amount of premium which can qualify is £2,000 for a married couple, ie £800 tax relief, or £1,000 for a single person, ie £400 tax relief. There are some restrictions: (a) the annual premium may not exceed 7% of the capital sum insured; (b) total qualifying premiums must not exceed 16.6%, ie one-sixth of your total income for tax purposes. If you do not already hold policies which use up your total life assurance relief, you can improve your family security or save for the rainy day by using this heading of tax relief. (As already mentioned, persons in an early stage of their mortgage should also look at this heading as a way of maximising their tax relief).

VHI — Medical Insurance Premiums — the full amount of premiums paid by the taxpayer on her own or her dependants' behalf to cover medical, hospital, or other illness expenses is deductible. The deduction granted is the premium paid in the previous year. For a high rate taxpayer this means that a premium of £100 in effect only costs £44. This relief is at present unrestricted as to the overall maximum amount of premiums.

Permanent Health Insurance — the full amount of premiums for permanent health insurance, ie insurance providing for periodic income payments in the event of the insured being unable to work through illness, is deductible. The amount deductible is restricted to 10% of total income and income paid under the policy will be subject to tax in the normal way.

Single Parent Allowance — where someone, either single or previously married, is caring for a child on a full-time basis, she/he is entitled to claim a single parent allowance of £2,050 per annum if deserted, separated or unmarried, or £1,550 if widowed. In this instance, the tax bands that apply will be those relevant to single persons.

Rent Allowance — a tenant aged 55 or more living in private rented accommodation is entitled to tax relief on the rent paid. Relief is given for rent payments made in the calendar year preceding the tax year; the maximum is £1,500 for a married couple and £750 for other persons. This relief should certainly be considered by older people, particularly married couples, who might be considering a change of home.

Age Allowance — an individual who is 65 years of age or over at any time in the tax year, including a married person who has opted for single assessment, is entitled to an additional age allowance of £200 per annum. Married couples who have opted for joint taxation and either of whom is 65 years or over at any time of the tax year are entitled to £400 per annum tax-free allowance.

Blind Person's Allowance — a blind single person, or married person who has opted for single taxation is entitled to an allowance of £600. In the case of a married couple who opt for joint taxation, the allowance is £600 where one spouse is blind or £1,400 where both spouses are blind.

Dependent Relative Allowance — where the taxpayer maintains at her own expense (a) an infirm relative of herself or her spouse or (b) her own or her spouse's widowed mother, whether or not infirm or (c) a son or daughter residing with her on whom she depends because she, the taxpayer, is infirm or incapacitated, the taxpayer is entitled to a dependent relative allowance of £110 in repect of each such dependent relative. A point that should be noted is that where a dependent relative has income, the amount of the dependent relative allowance in respect of that particular relative is reduced pound for pound by the excess of that income over the maximum rate of social welfare contributory old age pension (approximately £3,042 per annum).

Employer/Caretaker — where the taxpayer employs a person to care for her because she, or her spouse, is totally incapacitated by old age or infirmity, the taxpayer is entitled to a special allowance of £2,500.

Incapacitated Child — this allowance of £600 is granted to the parent of a physically or mentally handicapped child, usually where the handicap occurred before age 18.

These then are the main allowances which, if applicable to your situation, should appear on your tax-free allowance certificate.

Other Tax Reliefs

Medical Expenses — as you go through the year it is difficult to anticipate your likely medical expenses. However, as a general rule, you should certainly keep all receipts for any medical expenses, as you may be entitled to claim a tax refund for these at the year end. The important thing is to keep the receipts, so that you will have the necessary evidence to support your claim. A tax refund is obtainable for expenditure which is not reimbursed from another source (eg the VHI or a health board) and which is more than either £50 for a single person or £100 for a family. Qualifying expenses include outlays for medical, dental, and ophthalmic purchases but not for routine items such as normal maternity care, filling, extracting or cleaning of teeth, or eye tests. Claims can include costs of drugs, physiotherapy, home nursing, doctor's fees, ambulance charges, orthodontic treatment, etc, and the £10 a day hospital in patient charge and hospital out patient charges introduced in 1987/88. Relief is given at your marginal rate of tax, so £100 of qualifying medical expenses would mean a tax saving of £56 if you were a 56% taxpayer. There is also the option to claim on either a family basis or a single basis, depending on which is most to your advantage. For example, if you are in a family situation but most of your expenses relate to one individual in the family, it is probably a better idea to claim using the single exclusion of £50 rather than the family exclusion of £100. This means that your tax refund would be greater.

Occupational Expenses — you may belong to an occupational group which has a special allowance agreed with the Revenue Commissioners, such as nurses, printers and chefs. Do not assume that this allowance will come automatically; make sure that you claim it. In addition, if you have expenses which are wholly, exclusively and necessarily incurred in the performance of your duties and which are not reimbursed by your employer, these may be tax-deductible. They could include, for example, travel and subsistence costs, not reimbursed; the cost of tools used by yourself where you are required to supply them; or the cost of membership of a professional organisation where that membership is a condition of your employment and must be paid by you. Obviously, any expenses which are reimbursed by your employer do not qualify.

Covenants — a covenant is a legally binding promise in writing to make periodic payments without receiving anything in return. The person who pays the covenant is then regarded as having a lower total income, and hence a lower tax liability, and the person receiving the covenant is regarded as being in receipt of income which will be assessed for tax. There are restrictions on the amounts that persons can covenant to children and grandchildren, ie the total covenants to all persons in this category cannot exceed 5% of the donor's total income.

However, money paid to incapacitated children is not used in calculating this overall restriction. The amount that children can covenant to parents, or aunts to nieces, nephews, etc, is not restricted, but where the total amount of the covenant exceeds £10,000 (eg covenant of £2,000 per annum multiplied by seven years equals £14,000), capital taxes will arise, ie stamp duty and perhaps capital acquisitions tax.

Other Interest Relief — relief is available, in addition to normal mortgage interest relief, where a taxpayer incurs interest charges on funds used to buy shares or loan money to a company in which they are either employees or directors. Relief is also available where interest arises on money used to buy a share in a partnership. Where the person is a whole-time director or employee holding 5% or more of the ordinary share capital, interest relief is generally unrestricted. Where the person is a whole-time director or employee holding less than 5%, in the case of a private company, the relief is also unrestricted, but in the case of a public company interest relief is restricted to £2,400. Part-time directors and employees may also be eligible for this type of interest relief.

Business Expansion Scheme (BES) — this is a relief designed to encourage high earners and taxpayers to invest in certain types of Irish company. Monies invested must be used to purchase shares and the company must be involved in either manufacturing, certain types of services or more recently, certain areas of tourism. The company must not be listed on the Stock Exchange. Relief is available on amounts invested between £500 and £25,000 and is available at your highest rate of tax. The shares must be held for five years.

It goes without saying that this type of investment can be risky. However, because of the tax relief there is a limit on your exposure to the true cost of the shares in that tax relief reduces the cost by your marginal rate of tax. If you are a 56% taxpayer, therefore, the true cost of a £1 share to you is 44 pence. This allows a wide margin before you actually start to lose money.

Deductions — Benefit-in-Kind/Other Income

Now let us take a brief look at the other side of the coin, ie deductions from allowances. These can come under a variety of headings and include pensions, etc. The most common deduction is called *benefit-in-kind.* For example, if a taxpayer is in receipt of a company car, this benefit is assessed at 20% of the market price of the car when new. This assessment can be reduced down to 12%, depending on the payment by the taxpayer of certain types of motor expenses. If the taxpayer drives more than 25,000 miles per annum on business, this tax liability does not apply.

Share option schemes and VHI paid by your company will also be assessed as benefit-in-kind. Share options and share purchase schemes are complicated and it is a good idea to ask your employer what benefit-in-kind has been agreed with the Revenue Commissioners. You then return this when you are completing your annual tax return.

SUMMARY

- Although this general discussion of the tax system may appear quite complex at first glance, a reasonable grasp of how the system works can put you in more control and enable you to make sure that your tax affairs are up-to-date.
- Do make sure to check the figures on any tax-free allowances or assessments that you receive, and never assume that these figures are automatically right.
- The Revenue Commissioners have a certain amount of discretion as to how much of any particular expense they can allow, so where you are claiming for expenses, such as interest, always give the complete details and see what relief is allowed to you. If you feel that the relief is too low, do correspond with your Revenue Commissioners to see if you can come to some better arrangement.

SETTING UP IN BUSINESS

More and more people, and in particular women, are choosing to set up in business for themselves, for a variety of reasons. The need for independence is strong in some cases; others, because of our high PAYE rates, find that their net pay is low and feel that they could improve both their lifestyles and their finances by working for themselves.

Self-employment does offer considerable rewards, but there are few enough who make a fortune overnight! You will need to invest a number of years of very hard work before you can expect your business to be established. However, there is a lot that you can do at the beginning to see whether the venture is viable. Detailed advice on the subject is given in the companion guide **Business Matters For Women**, so I will only outline some of the major considerations you should keep in mind.

MOTIVATION

It is very important to *want* to be self-employed. That might seem obvious, but this option is not just a job, it is more a way of life. You should also have a strong interest in the area you intend to work in, particularly if it's a service that you will be delivering yourself. You should have good judgement and the ability to make decisions, and you must be able to deal with the anxiety that comes from the personal risk you are taking. Remember, you will be the sole determinant of your own income, and in the beginning this is likely to be meagre and probably irregular. Perhaps you can test the water gradually. Could you start your new career in your spare time, to see if it is viable, and when you have built up some regular income, make the move fully? Many women move gradually into self-employment. Sometimes a particular skill such as catering may develop into a full-time occupation; however, other areas may not be approached in this way. If possible, try to have either a certain amount of work pre-sold, or else have a financial nest egg sufficient to cover you for the first three to six months.

DOING YOUR FIGURES AND ASSESSING YOUR MARKET

The first question you should ask is 'how much money do I need to make to justify setting up in business?' Remember, you should value your time also, and put this into the equation. I find that unless they require borrowings, many would-be entrepreneurs do not cost out their business in any great detail. This is particularly so where you may be working from home and are offering a service rather than a physical product. Nevertheless, you should first try to estimate how much it is actually going to cost you to be in business, then add the cost of your time, to see what your minimum turnover should be.

Your main priority is to see if there is a *market* for your product or service at the price at which you can afford to sell it. Find out all you can about your competitors, and if possible try to have some idea of the size of the market you hope to tap. This can be a bit daunting, but if you at least know how many products or hours you need to sell to generate your required income, you can use this as your target. If you are going to manufacture a product, find out whether you need a licence to trade, or whether you should consider having your product patented if, for example, you feel your idea is original and could be copied. If you are going to be involved in manufacturing you should also approach the government agencies involved for grant aid or subsidies, eg the Industrial Development Authority.

In profit terms, it is very important to have some idea of your *break-even position*, ie the level of sales at which your business starts to make a profit. At its simplest, if you have total costs of £100 per month, and your product sells at £5, then you need to sell 20 units per month *before* you start to make any profit. If you are selling a time-related service, the same principle applies, ie how many hours do I have to work to cover my basic overheads? Have a good hard look at this break-even figure, either in service hours or number of units to be sold. If it looks unrealistic, you will have to re-examine your costs and pricing again.

THE LEGAL SIDE

This relates to the type of business structure that you choose to operate within, eg company or sole trader. Your main concern in deciding which option to choose is to protect yourself and your personal assets in the event of your business going wrong. You also want a structure that is flexible and does not have too many rules and regulations to fulfil, and which enables you to optimise your tax position.

Limited Company

If you are involved in manufacturing, it can be a good idea to opt for a limited company. This is because there is a higher risk factor in manufacturing, and you could need the protection of limited liability. In addition, you may also be able to qualify for corporation tax at 10%, and you may be able to raise money for development under the Business Expansion Scheme. However, information on your company will have to be filed on public record under new EC laws, and you must have your accounts audited, and comply with the many rules laid down by the Companies Act. This can be time-consuming and expensive. You should therefore be sure that the size and risk of your operation would justify the time and expense involved in setting up a limited company.

Sole Trader and Partnerships

If your operation is small, and the risks you are concerned about in the business can be covered by insurance, a sole trader or partnership structure might be more appropriate. These are more flexible and there are very few legal requirements. In fact, if you operate as a sole trader with your own name you do not even have to register. But do be careful if you are using some other trade name; you will have to register the trade name and get approval before you proceed. With the sole trader structure, your main responsibilities will relate to tax, ie income tax and VAT, and effectively you can start up your business with a minimum delay, ie as long as it takes you to get premises and printed stationery.

If you are going into partnership with someone, the situation is the same as with the sole trader. However, it is a very good idea to have a partnership agreement setting out your intentions as to how the partnership will work. This document should set out the initial investment of the partners, the duties and responsibilities of each partner, how the finances of the partnership will operate, eg salaries, fees, drawings, profits, and what would happen in the event of disagreement or death.

When drawing up the agreement spend some time

beforehand discussing precisely who will do what in relation to your business. Try to anticipate how the business will work so that you can see each partner's role clearly. You will also need to specify how partners are to rewarded, ie regular income and profits, and how this is to be related to the input in terms of time, money or expertise of each of the partners.

TAX AND YOUR BUSINESS

Depending on the structure of your business, you will pay income tax on profits if you are a sole trader or partnership, and corporation tax on profits if you are a company. Profits for a sole trader are added to other income and taxed accordingly. Losses in one's trade can be offset against other income and you may also be able to claim back tax paid in earlier years. The timing of your commencing date can have significant effects on your tax position, and your first year's profits/losses will normally be used as the basis for your first three years' assessments of tax. As well as income tax, you will have to pay levies and PRSI on your income up to the current limits. If you are a company you will pay corporation tax on your profit, either at 10% if you are a manufacturing company, or 43% for other companies with effect from March 1989. Profit that is distributed to directors or shareholders will receive a tax credit, ie the profit will have been tax paid at 35%. However, if you are a higher rate taxpayer, you will be liable for additional tax on the gross profit paid to you. In calculating profit of a company the gross income is used, less allowable expenses and capital expenses, to give profit before tax. The tax is then calculated at the appropriate rate and deducted, giving the profit for distribution. A loss made by the company cannot be used by the shareholders to offset tax due on other income, but it can be carried forward against future profits in the company.

PAYE, PRSI and VAT

The other main forms of taxation which you will find yourself involved with are PAYE, PRSI and VAT. If you employ people, either in a sole tradership or in a company, you are obliged to register as an employer and to deduct and remit PAYE and PRSI. If you manufacture VAT-rated goods worth more than £25,000 per annum, or expect to invoice for fees of more than £1,000 per month, you are obliged to register for VAT. Certain types of goods are zero-rated and if you think your turnover is likely to be in excess of the VAT thresholds, you should register and make the returns every two months. VAT returns will take account of the VAT that you have paid to your suppliers and the VAT that you have collected from your customers. It is the net amount between these two figures that you must pay to the Revenue Commissioners.

The important thing to remember is that employer's PRSI will cost you 12.13% of your employee's salary up to certain limits, which adds to your total costs. Equally, if you are obliged to charge VAT to your customer, this increases the cost to them of your goods or services. Where the customers are VAT-registered, they can offset the VAT they pay you against the VAT they themselves charge. However, if your customers are not VAT-registered, eg personal clients for services, the VAT charge may make the difference between whether you get the business or not. Nevertheless, if your turnover is above the limits, you have no option but to comply with the rules.

SUMMARY

- This is only a very brief summary of some of the points you need to consider if thinking about setting up in business. You should examine your overall financial situation and the business idea carefully and then obtain good professional advice.
- Money spent at the beginning in evaluating and organising your project to your best advantage will repay itself handsomely and will significantly improve your chances of success.
- There is, of course, a lot of work that you can do yourself in assessing your markets, and you should see what sort of research and financial information you can put together yourself before looking for professional advice.

SECTION 3 — THE DEADLINE DECADES

PLANNING FOR RETIREMENT

Most people hope to live a long and healthy life but, amazingly, relatively few take active steps to ensure that they have the financial resources to enjoy the golden years. If you are approaching 30, you should be thinking about your long-term future. Investing in a pension can be the best way to maximise your savings return, and save on tax immediately. Even if you are much closer to retiring age, don't let the fact that you have not made retirement plans before deter you from starting now — better late than never.

THE STATE PENSIONS

Whatever the nature of your employment, when you are paying full-rate PRSI contributions, you are building entitlement to a state contributory pension. Currently, the maximum personal rate is £58.50 per week or £95.80 per week for a married couple, assuming you are both under the age of 80.

However, there are a number of conditions that you must fulfil to qualify for this pension: you must have paid PRSI for ten years before retirement and, to qualify for a full pension, you must have 48 contributions per annum on average since you started work, ie entered insurable employment after 1953. You can qualify for a reduced pension, ie £50 per week, if your average is 20+ contributions per annum. At first glance these conditions may appear enough to meet, but in practice it often works out unfairly for the individuals concerned.

Although the state pensions give some financial protection providing you qualify, you really must consider whether you could live, in today's terms, on £50 to £58 per week. For most of us the answer would be 'no'.

PRIVATE PENSIONS

Overall Limits on Benefits

If you are working in permanent employment, your employer may operate a pension scheme. The rules about how much an employer can provide for you by way of pension benefit are laid down by the Revenue Commissioners and these rules are quite generous. They allow a company pension scheme to provide a full pension of two-thirds of final 'remuneration' ie salary, plus bonus, plus commission, plus benefit-in-kind, and also a dependants' (ie spouse and children) pension, in the event of your death before and after retirement. To qualify for full pension, you must have worked for a minimum of ten years. Alternatively you can substitute part of this full pension for a lump sum, which cannot exceed 1½ times final remuneration. In this case, your pension will be reduced. These benefits can be paid in addition to your state contributory pension.

Capital Required

These limits, as I have said, are quite generous. However, the main point to remember about pensions is that they are the very same in broad principle as any other form of savings. If you are to have an income of, say, £10,000 per annum and a lump sum of £30,000, there must be a fund of money available to provide this. In today's terms, for a woman of 60, there would need to be approximately £134,000 capital available. If she were 65, she would need £125,000 — the older you take a pension the less capital is required, because your life expectancy is less. Now think how long it could take to save £125,000 plus, and this will put pensions into perspective for you. Someone has to save this money, either you or your employer. Even if inflation stays at 5% for the next ten years, this will mean that you would need £218,000 if you are now 50, and plan to retire at 60, to provide a pension as outlined above. This would provide the equivalent of £10,000 per annum plus £30,000 lump sum in today's terms.

Investment Incentives

Although the amount of capital you need to provide to give you a comfortable retirement is large, there are strong incentives available for pensions in the form of tax relief. The best of these, in terms of contributions, are available to companies. Companies are allowed to contribute higher percentages of your salary, tax free, than you are. For example, a company could put 50% per annum of your salary, tax free, into pension on your behalf, assuming you are aged 45 next birthday. On the other hand, an individual is usually only allowed to invest 15% of their earnings each year. The effect of tax relief on both contributions is to reduce the real cost of the £1 investment by the company's and the individual's highest rate of tax. So for a company paying 43% corporation tax, £1 invested costs 57p, and for the individual paying 56p tax, £1 costs 44p.

In addition to the tax relief on the contributions, the cash invested is also treated favourably tax-wise. Ordinary investment funds are taxed at a rate of 35% on profits, whereas money invested in a pension fund is exempt from tax. This means that your money grows at a faster rate. Another important point about a company pension scheme is that, unlike other company benefits, there is no tax charge on the employee in terms of benefit-in-kind as a result of a company's contributions to your pension scheme.

COMPANY PENSION SCHEMES

If you are working for a company with a pension scheme, you should view this scheme as part of your remuneration and not as something that doesn't concern you. The way your particular scheme is arranged can have an effect on your retirement planning and you should study the company booklet and check out the details of your scheme carefully. Remember, your company is not obliged to provide you with a pension, and is not obliged to provide a scheme up to Revenue maximums.

Retirement Benefits

There are two ways of describing what your pension scheme might provide. One is where it is linked to final pay, ie your pension will be based on some proportion of your final salary and will depend on the number of years of service you have, eg 40 years' service. This arrangement is more common with large companies. The other method is where a particular percentage of your salary is invested, either by the company or by a combination of your own and the company's contributions. This money builds up in a fund which is used to provide a pension for you at the time you retire. The actual pension will depend on the investment returns available when you retire and cannot be specified at the beginning, although you can get an estimate. This is the method used for self-employed pensions but one which more companies are now also using.

With the first type, the definition of a number of terms will place overall limits on your benefits. You need to understand how these work, so let's look at an example:

Final Salary

(a) This can include bonus, commission, benefit-in-kind, and basic salary.
(b) More usually it will be defined as final basic salary.

Final Pensionable Salary

This could be (a) above, more usually it will be (b). It can also be defined as (b) less some multiple of the state pension, ie once or twice single rate contributory old age pension. This then is the basis on which your actual pension will be calculated. This third type of definition is what is known as an 'integrated scheme', ie the benefits take account of social welfare benefits that *may* be available to you.

Number of years service required for full pension:

(a) This can be as little as ten years.
(b) More usually it will be 40 years, so you would get one-sixtieth or one-eightieth of final pensionable salary for every year you'd worked.

Lump sum entitlement

(a) You could have entitlement to 1½ times remuneration after 20 years.

(b) More usually it will be three-eightieths of final pensionable salary for every years' service.

If you are in a scheme, examine your own definitions carefully and convert your maximum potential service at different retirement ages into today's money terms. If the figures look inadequate, see whether there is any way you could improve your position. Perhaps you are only putting in 5% of salary, or perhaps your employer is contributing all the premiums? You could get tax relief on premiums up to 15% of salary, so check if you can invest some extra money in your own pension by way of an additional voluntary contribution. Also check what this extra contribution would be likely to provide in terms of pension at retirement.

OPTIONS IF YOU LEAVE EMPLOYMENT

In today's employment market, it may happen that you change employment a number of times and find yourself moving from pension scheme to pension scheme. What are your options in this instance? Again, the Revenue Commissioners lay down the main guidelines for this situation. They are as follows:

1. You can take a refund of your own contributions with or without interest, subject to 10% tax;
2. You can take a deferred pension, based on your years of service and your salary on leaving, which may or may not be indexed between leaving and final retirement, or
3. A transfer value may be paid into the scheme of your new employer.

For the third option to operate, your new employer and your old employer would both have to have company pension schemes, and your previous employer would have to be able to assess the value of all contributions to date to provide a transfer value. This option would usually be the best way to maintain realistic pension benefits, but it is seldom available. Option two, if you have any length of time to go to retirement, can be worth very little and often does not allow for indexation. Option one, therefore, is the most usually selected. However, where this option has been exercised, the usual tendency is to spend the money refunded, or to use it for some other short-term requirement. If this happens a couple of times, it is quite easy to find yourself in your middle years with no pension entitlement whatever.

MONEY PURCHASE SCHEMES

The alternative to company final pay pension schemes is what is know as 'money purchase schemes'. In this type of scheme, your money (and the company's contributions, if you are in an occupational scheme) is invested and grows as you proceed towards retirement. If you're in a company scheme, what you finally get will still be subject to the Revenue Commissioners' overall maximums, ie two-thirds of final remuneration, etc. However, you won't know what the investment will be worth until retirement, when your fund is valued and your pension determined. The investment qualifies for tax relief in the normal way. The individual characteristics of employees can be taken into account in company schemes operated like this, so that a higher percentage contribution may perhaps be made for older employees with a shorter time to retirement. Where the time to retirement is shorter, this means that more money will need to be saved to provide realistic benefits.

SELF-EMPLOYED PENSIONS

For self-employed persons, 'money purchase' is the only approach to pension provision available and is the most realistic, as it is impossible to know what income you might have between now and retirement. Unlike occupational schemes, self-employed pensions are not restricted to the two-thirds rule and the only revenue requirement is that 25% of the fund value may be taken in the form of tax-free cash, with the balance being used to provide a pension which will be taxable in the normal way.

SUMMARY

- If you're working and are a member of an occupational scheme, look at the scheme details to see what it will provide. If it is not adequate, see if you can improve it or could save for retirement in some additional way.
- If you're working but have no pension scheme, see if your employer is prepared to contribute to one, and if so arrange to make contributions yourself as well.
- If your employer is not prepared to contribute, set up your own scheme and contribute as much as you can afford. You will get relief on 15% of your earnings each year but can contribute more to a self-employed pension if you wish.

- If you're likely to change jobs frequently in developing your career, consider setting up your own scheme anyway. It may be possible to get your employer to contribute also, but you have the advantage of your pension being totally portable, ie it will move with you from job to job.
- If you're not in paid employment, you cannot undertake a pension *per se*. You can, however, invest in other forms of long-term savings and could get tax relief on these also.
- Unfortunately because of women's traditional place in the workforce and the home, they have fared badly in regard to pensions and often find themselves with little or no entitlement as they approach middle and later life. Pensions, as I have already said, are savings and can be provided for either through the offical pension route or through other forms of savings and investment. Knowing that you can look forward to some form of financial independence in later life is extremely important to most people's sense of well being. Whether you are working or not, don't neglect this crucial aspect of your financial plan.

SEPARATION

Proposed legislation that is currently under review will have a significant impact on the lives of many separated couples. It may enable persons in a broken marriage to obtain a decree of separation on a no-fault basis after three years, and to have the matter of succession dealt with in a conclusive manner. However, many people do not have recourse to the courts where their marriage breaks down and may instead draw up their own separation agreement. For this to be legal, they must have it completed by a solicitor and can have it ruled in the courts, should they wish. Where no agreement is reached, and/or in the case of desertion, it is essential to consult a solicitor as early as possible. The whole area is extremely complex, involving as it does law and the ownership of assets, tax and finance. The following points do not presume to cover the area in any comprehensive way, but rather aim at outlining the major areas of consideration for anyone finding themselves in this situation.

When faced with the prospect or reality of separation, you will need to consider what is likely to happen under the following headings:

1. Income — will there be maintenance involved, or are you entitled to social welfare payments?
2. Home — Will you continue to live where you are, and what share or entitlement do you have?
3. Property — Are there any other assets that you need to deal with, eg savings, business, life assurance, etc. and to whom do these belong?
4. Children — who will care for them, how will this be paid for, where will they live?
5. Death — what would you now like to happen to your own and your partner's assets in the event of the death of either?

In a separation agreement, all these issues will have to be discussed and as far as possible agreed. Where desertion occurs, the matters may have to be ruled in court but in respect of maintenance and succession, certain rules may apply. Where one partner deserts and this is the case for two years before the death of the other spouse, the right of succession would be lost. A deserting partner can also lose the right to maintenance from the other partner. Adultery can sometimes cause the loss of entitlement to maintenance.

INCOME

This may be in the form of maintenance from an ex-spouse, or social welfare benefit, or allowance arising from desertion. You may also be working and earning an income and this would usually exclude you from receiving deserted social welfare allowance. It does not, however, exclude you from receiving deserted benefit or maintenance, although there will be tax implications for your overall income. The conditions for eligibility for deserted spouse's benefit or allowance are outlined in the **Social Welfare for Women Handbook**. Where there are children, you will also continue to receive children's allowance.

Maintenance can be either agreed or awarded by the court. Where there are children, the figure will usually be allocated partly to the spouse and partly to the children and there may also be conditions laid down for a review of the figures, eg when children reach a certain age, or when the spouse receiving the maintenance becomes financially independent. In arriving at a figure for maintenance, it is essential to detail all the expenses that are to be covered, and where you would be applying to the courts, it is also necessary to have these expenses vouched, ie receipts, bills, etc. To assess properly how much maintenance might be awarded or agreed, you will need to have full information on both partners' financial affairs and legal procedures can be used to obtain this information. Redundancy monies or pension lump sums would not be considered part of the means in assessing how much maintenance should be awarded. If you are claiming maintenance, and the overall figure would include your budget for bills, etc., it is a good idea to have the total figure paid to you directly, rather than continue to have an ex-spouse pay for these items. By paying the bills yourself, you have much more control of the situation.

Maintenance payments can either be tax-free or taxable, depending on the tax situation of both partners. It is now possible to opt for joint but separate taxation where a legal separation agreement exists, and this can confer some tax benefits to the couple which are not available if they are taxed as single people. To decide which option might suit best, a full analysis of each person's tax situation would need to be carried out. Maintenance that is paid in respect of children, however, is usually deemed to be 'tax paid' so no further liability would arise on this portion of the overall payment. If you opt for joint separate assessment, you would not be entitled to a single parent allowance. Where single assessment is chosen, it may be possible for both partners to claim single parent's allowance, as well as their personal allowance, depending on the arrangements made between them with regard to caring for the children. When agreeing a maintenance figure, it is also important to consider whether this should be indexed in the future.

FAMILY HOME

Under the Family Home Protection act, it is usually not possible to sell the property without the consent of both spouses. However, unless the property is held jointly, this does not mean that ownership is automatically 50/50. Where a home was held in single title, the other spouse would have to apply to the courts to have their share entitlement ruled and they would usually have to prove that they had contributed to the purchase of the home. There is, however, a case under review at the time of writing where a share of the family home has been awarded to a wife who could not prove a monetary contribution; if this decision is upheld in the Supreme Court there will be wide-ranging legal implications for many separated couples.

It is also possible to negotiate a share of the family home without proceeding to the courts. Generally speaking, unless a share has been negotiated or awarded it is not a good idea to agree to sell the family home, provided no other pressure to sell applies. This is because there are laws which can protect the family home and a spouse's entitlement to live there, which will not apply to other properties. Where there are mortgage arrears, protection of the home may not be possible, so it is wise to assess immediately whether there are any debts outstanding on the property. If necessary, you should approach the lender directly to find out the up-to-date situation, but unless you are in a position to pay arrears, the lender can proceed to have the property sold. It is possible to obtain a court order to have arrears paid, but this will obviously depend on your spouse's financial situation. It is also possible to obtain a maintenance order, even where a couple are not separated, and in this case an attachment would be put on the spouse's salary and could be used to pay a mortgage or other debts directly.

When negotiating or proceeding legally to obtain an agreement regarding a separation, it is vitally important to resolve the issue of the family home, ie ownership, share, and security of tenure. If there is a mortgage, it must continue to be paid. If the home is purchased from the local authority it is important to be aware that on the sale of the property, the authority will usually require both parties to declare that they will not require public housing in the future. A further important point regarding the local authority is that if you render yourself deliberately homeless, you will not usually be entitled to alternative public housing.

SUCCESSION

The legal provisions regarding succession are currently under review. For the moment, however, you would need to consider the issue and if possible agree what would happen in the event of either person's death. There are certain situations where succession entitlement would cease, eg desertion, or a decree of judicial separation. However, for many people neither of these situations might be applicable, so the issue of succession can remain open unless resolved between them.

The waiving of succession rights obviously has considerable long term implications. This may be considered where an acceptable separation agreement regarding maintenance and the disposal of other assets, eg family home, savings, etc. is reached. Where agreement is not possible, these rights would not usually be waived and this means that each spouse continues to be entitled to a share of the other's estate after death. It goes without saying that you will need to review the arrangements of your will after separation.

SUMMARY

- It is essential to obtain advice, both legal and financial, if you find yourself facing separation for any reason.
- If possible, try to resolve the various issues between you and be aware of the present and long-term implications.
- Where you cannot agree, you may have no alternative but to have the matter resolved through the courts. This will normally take quite some time and will usually involve legal costs.

DEATH OF A PARTNER

Anyone facing this situation will require emotional and professional support from a number of people. Initially the difficulty can be just to cope with the situation, but there are a number of things that must be dealt with to ensure that the process complies with legal and state requirements. Thereafter, to sort out the estate and to enable you to manage financially, there are further courses of action. My intention in this section is to outline briefly what you can expect to face. I would also counsel you to seek assistance from friends and professionals who will help you through this difficult period.

If your partner dies at home, the first person you should contact is your family doctor; she/he will advise you as to the proper procedure. If the doctor was attending your partner in their final illness, she/he will provide you with a death certificate and will explain to you how to register the death. If your partner died unexpectedly, or as a result of an accident or violence or injury, the death will usually be reported to the coroner, who may decide to hold an inquest into the cause of death. This would usually involve a postmortem, for which your permission would be required, and the results would be reported to the coroner. This process may take a few days, and there may be a preliminary hearing for identification purposes only. After this, the body is released for burial.

Between death and burial, you may find out the conditions of your partner's will, if there is one. The will states who the executors are, perhaps yourself, a close friend or relative, or a solicitor. You should seek the assistance and support of these people in making the funeral arrangements. Try to have an estimate of costs. At this stage you will need to see where funds will be provided from. If you have funds of your own, you can use these, or if you operated a joint account, there may be sufficient funds in this account to meet immediate expenses. Funeral expenses are normally met ultimately by the estate, but this money may not be forthcoming until probate is granted, and this could take some time. If you have no funds available and fulfil certain PRSI conditions, you may be able to claim a death grant of £100. If the death occurred because of an accident at work, you may be eligible for a funeral grant of £220. You must claim either of these grants within three months of the date of death and if you are entitled to them you could probably get an advance on these funds from your bank in the form of a loan. The undertaker will explain to you the burial procedures and you will usually need to sign some papers for the cemetery.

After the funeral, you should examine the will in detail, if there is one. If no will has been made, you should select a personal representative to help you administer the estate. The rules governing how the estate is to be administered, where there is, or is not, a will, are set out in Chapter 9. Where there is a will you need to check the position of the remaining spouse, if any, to see if it complies with the law. I make this point because many people in Ireland may find themselves dealing with a partner's death where they are not in fact the legal 'spouse'. Otherwise, the estate should be distributed according to the dead person's instructions. Where there is no will, the estate would be divided according to the rules of intestacy. However, this does not mean that those entitled to benefit cannot waive part of their inheritance in favour of someone else, if they so wish.

The procedure involved in applying for probate or letters of administration can be quite time consuming and if one of the executors is a solicitor she/he would usually handle this, for which she/he may charge fees. As a start, you should certainly inform the bank, insurance companies, mortgage company, employer company, any other savings or investments institutions, and also any people to whom money was owed. You should try to get a clear idea of the value of all assets, and also all liabilities, as these will be required for probate. If your partner was in a pension scheme, and if you were married, you should see whether there is a spouse's pension available and what is required to enable the payment of this to you. The timing of this payment may sometimes be at the discretion of your partner's previous employer and may not always require a grant of probate or letters of administration. Having done this much, I would certainly consult a solicitor, unless the value of the estate is very small. Even if you wish to administer the matter fully yourself, seek legal advice at some stage to ensure that you are handling it correctly. You should usually allow up to one year for the whole process, ie probate request, outstanding claims etc, to be resolved. Naturally there are many circumstances where the time taken to resolve the issue can be shorter.

Ongoing financial implications will vary widely depending on the financial provisions made prior to the death of the partner.

THE STATE BENEFITS

In the past, under the state system, women were treated more favourably than men in that there were contributory and non-contributory widow's pensions which were not generally available to widowers. Following a recent budget, benefits available to women in the form of widow's pensions and deserted wife's benefits will now also be available to men.

Widow's Contributory Pension — this is based on either her own or her husband's contributions to the date of death and is not affected by any other income or pension she may have, although it is included for tax purposes. The PRSI requirements, on one or other individual, are:

1. There must be at least 56 contributions paid to the date of death; and
2. Either (a) an average of 39 weeks paid or credited over the three or five tax years before the partner died, or reached pension age, ie 66, or (b) for minimum pension, a yearly average of at least 24 weeks paid or credited since starting work.

The difference between minimum and maximum pension is about £6.50 per week for the individual. Increases are available over the personal rate for dependent children.

Widow's Non-Contributory Pension — this may be available where PRSI is insufficient or non-existent, and this payment will be means-tested. The rate is £47.60 per week, with increases for dependent children.

Lump sums arising from partner's death, ie life insurance/death-in-service benefits — this would become available directly to the survivor where she/he is the joint policy owner, nominated beneficiary, or single policy owner of the particular policy. In the case of a joint life first death policy, the benefit would be paid on production of the death certificate. Where the deceased was insured for the benefit of the other partner and this is noted on the policy, benefit would be paid immediately on production of the death certificate. Where the deceased was insured 'in trust', the benefit would also pass on the death certificate, to the beneficiaries. However, where the deceased specified no beneficiaries and effected the insurance on themselves, probate will be required before the benefit is released. If the living partner had effected the insurance on the dead partner, probate would not be required to release the funds as the surviving partner would be, in effect, the policy owner. However, where a couple may have been separated, the original proposer would still be the owner of the policy, even if the deceased had always paid the premiums and might not have intended this money to go to the separated spouse. This is a point to note when reviewing your financial arrangements on separation.

In many cases, therefore, life assurance benefits will be paid quite quickly and this money should be placed in a high-earning interest account until the estate is administered and all bequests, debts and expenses are paid. Any balance could then be invested to produce an income for the remaining partner, or invested for purposes of capital growth. It should go without saying that if you receive a lump sum benefit of any size on the death of your partner this will preclude you, initially at least, from receiving a widow's non-contributory pension. For a widow with three children, a lump sum benefit of £53,500 would in most circumstances completely preclude her from a non- contributory widow's pension.

Pension Payable From Employment

This will vary depending on the conditions of the employer's scheme, but it is often 50% to 66% of the pension the deceased would have received, had she/he retired at the usual retirement date. There may also be a provision for children's, pension either inclusive or exclusive of the spouse's pension. This is another situation where there may be some discrimination in favour of women, in that private schemes may have widow's pension but not widower's — you should check this feature on your own and your partner's scheme. Pensions paid to surviving spouses will be assessed for tax in the normal way and some tax may be deducted at source by the employer.

TAX AND DEATH

Capital Tax

When a couple is married, either spouse is allowed to receive an unlimited amount from the deceased partner without having to pay tax. Children are allowed to receive up to £150,000 in total without liability to tax. If, however, partners were not married and there is a lump sum left to the survivor, amounts over £10,000 will be subject to tax. This is because of the Revenue Commissioners' view of the relationship as 'unconnected', as couples cannot divorce and remarry in Ireland. The rates of tax and the various thresholds for the different rates have been previously outlined in Chapter 9.

Income Tax

In the year of death double allowances may be given to the remaining spouse, and thereafter they will revert to widowed or single parent tax allowances, ie £2,550 per annum (widowed) or £4,100 per annum (single parent allowance). If the couple had been married they would have been able to avail of the double bands for tax purposes. However, when the partner dies, the survivor reverts to single bands. This basically means that the first £6,100 of taxable income would be taxed at 32%, the next £3,100 at 48% and the balance at 56%.

SUMMARY

- It can take weeks and months to come to grips emotionally with the loss of a partner. This is hardly the time when one wants to consider finances. Unfortunately, financial matters cannot be shelved and will keep requiring your attention.
- After a reasonable time has elapsed, say six months, you should try to review your financial situation. You may find that your income has fallen drastically.
- Check to see if you are entitled to any additional social welfare, or indeed that you are getting what you are eligible for. If you have received a lump sum, but have no other income, see if you can obtain a reduced widow's pension.
- Do not be tempted to spend all your capital but rather invest it wisely. You will require this financial fallback for your future.
- If your partner had been working, you may be experiencing the loss of this income and where there are children and perhaps large outgoings, this can be very difficult. Check to see if you are entitled to a contributory pension, either from the state or your partner's employer. Remember that this would be added to your other income for tax purposes, but

you can arrange to have this put on your tax-free allowance certificate so that you don't face a tax bill at the end of the year.

- If you are working, be sure to inform the Revenue Commissioners of your new situation so that you can keep your tax affairs straight.
- It may be that you are quite well-off after your partner's death, although this will not compensate for the loss. However, in time, financial security could enable you to take up new opportunities and will certainly assist you with the harsher day-to-day realities.
- Men who have lost a spouse who managed the home and children may frequently find themselves quite badly hit, although their own income may continue. This is because they may now have to employ someone to care for the children and home, and their net take-home pay will decrease, because of the move to single tax bands. It is therefore essential to ensure that there is adequate life assurance on the home-maker, as the loss of this person can have significant negative financial implications.

LUMP SUM INVESTMENT

On retirement, following redundancy, on the death of a partner or close relative, or indeed a win in the National Lottery, people may find themselves in receipt of a lump sum of money. This can be either tax free, or in the case of redundancy may be taxable. If you find yourself in this situation you need to carefully evaluate the range of options open to you for this money, depending on your family circumstances and on the tax and social welfare implications of the money. After careful consideration, you will be in a position to decide how to use this cash to give you the best benefit in your own particular circumstances.

REDUNDANCY

Lump sums on redundancy are more likely to happen where people are in their middle or later years. This situation requires very careful consideration, as the possibility of gaining future employment may be slim. Such a lump sum could be used to set up in a business, or invested for growth or income. Initially, if made redundant, you may be entitled to unemployment benefit, but this will cease after approximately fifteen months. If employment has not been attained at that stage, you may be entitled to unemployment assistance, but this will be means-tested, and any lump sum benefit that you are still holding will reduce your entitlement to unemployment assistance. For a single person on urban unemployment assistance of £39 per week, a lump sum of £20,000 would categorise them as having weekly means of £30 per week; their assistance would be reduced to £9 per week approximately. The same reduction would occur in married rate unemployment assistance but, where eligible, adult and children dependant rates could continue to be paid.

In my experience, the result of the way in which means are assessed for unemployment assistance is to force people to spend their redundancy lump sums so as to be eligible for the weekly assistance. This effectively wipes out the financial security of these individuals and leaves them totally dependent on the state for income.

SOURCES OF LUMP SUMS

The receipt of a lump sum from different sources has different tax implications:

1. **Redundancy monies** are subject to tax on amounts of over £6,000. Sometimes this figure may be increased to £10,000 by way of a calculation which is known as 'top slicing relief'. Your employer would normally get clearance for this in advance from the Revenue Commissioners so as to be in a position to apply any additional reliefs to your lump sum. You may be eligible for further tax reliefs, depending on your overall tax situation, and these should be claimed immediately after the end of the tax year in which you were made redundant.
2. Sums paid under *life assurance* contracts will be free of capital gains and income tax *per se* but may give rise to capital acquisition tax depending on who is in receipt of the money (see Chapter 9 for details).
3. **Retirement lump sums**, up to certain maximums, are free of tax, ie in occupational schemes 1½ times final remuneration and in self-employed pensions 25% of the value of the retirement fund.

INVESTMENT CONSIDERATIONS FOR LUMP SUMS

A number of considerations need to be examined before deciding how to proceed. The first of these, as with most financial decisions, is the *level of risk* that you will find acceptable. The second is the *rate of return* that you hope to make, which is strongly influenced by your choice of risk, and your tax position. The third is how *accessible* you want your money to be, ie can you get your money immediately or is there a fixed or desirable time span which you must leave before making withdrawals. Apart from these general considerations, the main question you should ask regarding a cash lump sum is 'what do I want this money to do for me?'. Your answer will indicate something about the time span for which you want to leave your investment, whether you want it to give you an income immediately or in the future, and the returns you will expect, relative to your degree of acceptable risk.

The following range of options is open to you:

Bank and Building Society Deposits

For lump sums, commercial banks and buildings societies offer the best rate of gross interest. Money can be placed on demand deposits or for a fixed term, eg one month, three months, six months or one year. Interest rates will vary on demand accounts in line with general interest rates, whereas money on a fixed interest deposit will guarantee a rate for the period chosen. Usually slightly higher rates of interest are paid for increasing sizes of lump sums. These types of deposits can be structured to provide a regular income facility.

Longer Term Fixed Deposits

Where a longer term of investment is possible, there are now one to five year fixed term accounts available from some building societies. The return is fixed at the outset and one can either have all the interest paid as income, or a portion, with the balance of interest paid as a bonus at the end of the investment term. Income can be paid monthly, quarterly, half-yearly or annually and the rates vary, with slightly higher rates paid where income is only paid annually. An alternative deposit investment, where no income is required, is to opt for growth and again a fixed return is available, with the term of the investment specified at the outset.

These longer-term fixed investments, unlike ordinary fixed term deposits and instant access accounts, are inflexible in that one cannot withdraw the bulk of the capital before the maturity date, unless in the case of death. This is not the case with the accounts discussed in Chapter 4, although you may incur an interest penalty on these when early withdrawal is made. Nor is it the case with investment alternatives, such as post office schemes, government securities or non guaranteed unit linked funds.

The Post Office

There are two investment options available from the post office — indexed-linked savings bonds and savings certificates. Post office investments are state guaranteed and therefore offer an excellent degree of security on investment. Returns on post office investments are also free of all forms of tax.

Index Linked Bonds

As the name suggests, index-linked bonds are guaranteed to increase the value of your investment in line with inflation for at least three years. At the end of the three years, there is an additional fixed bonus of 3% of the original sum invested. Present rates, includings the bonus, are 6.4% per annum for a three year term.

Savings Certificates

These certificates also offer a tax-free return of 40% after five years or the equivalent of 7% per annum for the full five year term. Minimum investment is £10, maximum is £25,000 per individual. Interest is added to the value of your investment at six monthly intervals, and the rate of interest rises the longer the investment is held, up to a full term of five years. Because of this rising rate over the term, the single annual rate goes from 5½% in the first year to an effective 8½% in the fifth year. However, the average annual rate of return is 7% over five years, and this is the figure to be used in any comparison with alternatives.

Government Securities

There is a wide range of government stocks, or gilts, which give a guaranteed return in terms of dividends/interest and the opportunity for tax-free capital growth. Government stocks are loans raised by the government with fixed redemption dates and interest rates and represent a very secure form of investment. Interest is fixed at an annual rate and is paid half-yearly without deduction of tax. Interest is, however, taxable so the net returns on annual payments will depend on your tax rate. As well as a regular interest payment, you may make a capital gain or loss by selling your stock at a higher or lower price than you paid for it. Gains made in this way are free of tax. In calculating the gross redemption yields on stock, which are quoted in the paper each week, both the interest and the capital gains are used, in relation to the price on the day, to give this measure of overall return.

Gilts are particularly suited to investors who are willing to hold the stock to maturity and who require a steady income and are low or non-taxpayers. They can provide either a regular guaranteed income or, once bought, a guaranteed level of growth (assuming they are purchased below the nominal level of the stock and are held to maturity). Additional capital gains can be made where prices of stock go above par price, eg £110 for £100 of stock, and any capital gains will be free of tax.

Guaranteed Income and Growth Bonds

Income Bond — guaranteed income bonds involve the payment of a lump sum to an insurance company which guarantees to pay the policy holder a certain income, quarterly, half-yearly or annually, for a fixed period. Income is paid over the investment term and the capital is then returned in full at the end of the period. The minimum investment is usually £3,000 and the term will vary from three to seven years. Income is not subject to tax, which makes these bonds particularly attractive to high taxpayers.

Growth Bonds — these bonds operate in a very similar way to income bonds, but the returns are added to the investment to give a guaranteed level of capital growth at the end of the investment term. As with Income Bonds, your investment is locked in for the full term so you need to be sure that you will not require your capital, or any part of the growth, in the meantime. Present rates for income bonds are 4.35% per annum over five years, or 24.25% growth after five years.

A purchased life annuity — is a personal annuity which you can buy from any life assurance company on a voluntary basis. It is a personal arrangement and although annuities are often linked to pensions, eg the pension fund may be used to buy an annuity, anyone with a lump sum can consider setting up this arrangement for themselves. You pay your lump sum to the life office and in return they pay you a regular income for an agreed period, eg your life. On your death, the annuity usually ceases and no capital sum, generally speaking, will be refunded. Annuities will usually only be considered by older people who want a regular fixed income or whose income is only required for a specified period.

Present single person annuity rates (capital: invested, for life, with no guarantees or escalation are as follows:

Woman 65 exactly — £10.79 per 1,000
Man 65 exactly — £12.29 per 1,000
Income paid monthly in advance.

This type of investment is most suitable for an older person with no dependants, and in that instance the rates of return can be quite good. Remember, however, that on death the annuity usually stops, so you should not consider an annuity if you are in poor health or do not expect to live a normal life span.

Unit Linked Funds/Capital Investment Bonds

These investments are operated and managed by life assurance companies in Ireland. They should not be confused with unit trusts, operated by the Bank of Ireland, which have very different tax treatment from unit-linked funds. When you invest in a *unit-linked fund*, or *capital investment bond* as they are often called, your money buys units in the fund of your choice, managed by the assurance company. Funds available cover different types of investments, eg *equity funds* will invest 100% in ordinary shares, *gilt funds* will invest in government funds and other fixed interest securities, *property funds* will invest in office blocks, factories and shops, *cash funds* will invest in short-term money markets, and *international funds* will invest in overseas markets. Rates of return on unit-linked funds are not guaranteed, although it is possible to guarantee the initial capital investment in some of the newer funds. Performance differs from company to company and also between the various funds, eg equity funds will generally produce higher returns in the three to five year period than gilt funds. Gains made from capital investment bonds are free of capital and income taxes.

SUMMARY

- If faced with the prospect of investing a lump sum, you should seek independent advice which will enable you to compare the various returns available at the time. For any reasonable sums of money, you should also seek to spread your investment risk and have money invested in guaranteed accessible products, as well as more medium-term investments geared towards higher returns.
- Time is a critical element in choosing your investment mix and you should always have a guaranteed accessible emergency fund available, which will be your first financial fallback.
- By having money available in short-term investments, such as building societies and banks, you are far more likely to leave your medium-term investments for the optimum period. This strategy will ensure that your money works in the most effective and profitable way, and is one that you can use in managing your regular income as well as larger sums of money.